THE
VIKING
HONDBÓK

THE
VIKING
HONDBÓK

EAT, DRESS, AND FIGHT *like a* WARRIOR

KJERSTI EGERDAHL

Running Press
PHILADELPHIA

Running Press
Hachette Book Group
1290 Avenue of the Americas, New York, NY 10104
www.runningpress.com
@Running_Press

Printed in China

First Edition: May 2020

Published by Running Press, an imprint of Perseus Books, LLC, a subsidiary of Hachette Book Group, Inc. The Running Press name and logo is a trademark of the Hachette Book Group.

The Hachette Speakers Bureau provides a wide range of authors for speaking events. To find out more, go to www.hachettespeakersbureau.com or call (866) 376-6591. The publisher is not responsible for websites (or their content) that are not owned by the publisher.

Print book cover and interior design by Paul Barrett and Rachel Marek
Produced by Girl Friday Productions

Library of Congress Control Number: 2019949764

ISBNs: 978-0-7624-9589-4 (hardcover), 978-0-7624-9587-0 (ebook)

RRD-S

10   9   8   7   6   5   4

CONTENTS

INTRODUCTION. **1**

I. THE VILLAGE: HOME AND WORK. **5**

A Viking Home 6

Viking Families. 9

The Look for Men 12

The Look for Women 16

Farming the Fjords and Fjells 20

Hunting and Fishing 23

Eat Like a Jarl 25

A Viking Brew 29

Honey and Mead: Nectar of the Gods 34

Weaving and Sewing 38

The Viking Tool Chest 43

II. THE KINGDOM: SOCIAL LIFE 47

Feasts and Festivals. 48

Grooming 51

Beards. 54

Women's Hair. 58

Jewelry 61

Drinking Customs 66

Weddings. 68

Games and Sports 74

Epic Poetry 77

King After King 79

III. THE VIKINGS ABROAD: SAILING TO NEW

WORLDS. 87

Boatbuilding 88

On the Water 95

Navigation. 99

Raiders and Warriors. 103

The King's English, or the Viking's?. 108

War Stories: Truth and Myths 110

Ragnar and the Blood Eagle 116

Weaponry 123

How Russia Got Its Name 130

Traders and Merchants 132
Explorers and Settlers 136
West to Iceland 139
Across the North Atlantic 150

IV. VALHALLA: GODS AND THE AFTERLIFE. . . 165

The World of the Gods 166
Odin 168
Thor 170
Frey and Freyja 175
Other Gods and Goddesses 178
Everything but the Hobbits 182
Pagan Rituals. 184
Ragnarök: The Downfall of the Gods. 193

APPENDICES: LEARN MORE 199

Appendix I. Timeline 200
Appendix II. The New Vinland: Viking Road Trip. . . . 204
Appendix III. Top Viking Museums 211
Appendix IV. Further Reading. 215

VIKING SETTLEMENTS

Norwegian Sea

ICELAND

SWEDEN

FINLAND

Atlantic Ocean

NORWAY

Baltic Sea

North Sea

DENMARK

IRELAND

BRITAIN

Just some of the areas Vikings had settled between the 9th and 11th centuries.

INTRODUCTION

Scandinavian Americans have been loud and proud about their Viking ancestors for a long time, and why shouldn't they be? Sure, these forebearers could sometimes be loudmouthed barbarians, puffed up with flash and swagger, who loved knocking heads (and knocking boots), but they also wrote epic poetry, brewed excellent beer, were skilled craftspeople and accomplished merchants, and mastered the lore of the sea. Vikings stayed loyal to the death, bonding over good food (well, good by premedieval standards) and good mead. The Vikings were a curious, resourceful group of global explorers, men and women alike, who approached new lands as raiders, yes, but also as traders and immigrants.

My own ancestors came to the United States as immigrants from Norway and Sweden, most of them several generations back. But my strongest Scandinavian influence comes from my grandfather Ottar Egerdahl, who came through Ellis Island as a child in the 1920s, lived briefly in South Dakota, and settled in Seattle, Washington.

Growing up, my grandfather and his siblings weren't allowed to speak Norwegian at home, only English, to help them assimilate. With a sense that something precious had been lost, my father, Ed, studied Norwegian as a young man, taking several trips to Norway and eventually founding the Scandinavian Language Institute, an organization that teaches language lessons through the National Nordic Museum in Seattle. I took all the kids' classes and a few adult sessions, but today my language skills hover somewhere between tourist quality and singing "Jeg er så glad" at Christmas.

One of the highlights of our family vacations was visiting the tiny northern valley of Egerdal in Nordland, where Ottar's family originated (the H in our last name was tacked on at Ellis Island). My dad was pretty excited when I married a man who knows how to make better *krumkake* than I do. But my main claim to fame is being a Sons of Norway parade princess as a senior in high school, waving to the crowd from the back of a convertible in the Norwegian Constitution Day parade. Kjersti the Viking Princess: carve that in runes on my tombstone.

I've always been inspired by the fierce, imaginative, adventurous legacy of the Vikings as it's come down to me in stories and through pop culture. We know the Vikings wove the perfect beard braid and built unstoppable warships, but who were these mysterious seafarers, really, and what were their everyday lives like? There's got to be more to it than the Marvel Comics superhero Thor lets on.

In the following pages, I've pulled together archaeological evidence, Norse writings, and foreign perspectives from the Viking Age to help answer these questions and to provide an informative, full, and—I hope—fun view of life as a Viking. After all, each of us could use a little more adventure in our lives. Here's hoping Odin, god of inspiration, spreads some of his magic to you.

—Kjersti-Marie Ragnhild Egerdahl
Seattle, WA
2020

BITTER IS THE WIND TONIGHT
IT TOSSES THE OCEAN'S WHITE HAIR.
TONIGHT I FEAR NOT THE FIERCE
WARRIORS OF NORWAY
COURSING THE IRISH SEA.
—Unknown Irish poet

I

THE
VILLAGE

HOME AND WORK

A VIKING HOME

Down on the Farm

During the Viking Age, most Scandinavians lived in small villages made up of six to eight farms—towns were relatively rare. Each farm had a longhouse as the main dwelling, surrounded

Enthusiastic seafarers, Vikings built longhouses shaped like a ship's hull.

by outbuildings like stables and storehouses and enclosed with a fence. Blacksmith shops, a fire hazard, usually stood at the edge of the property.

A typical longhouse had curved walls and an arched roofline like an upturned boat—everything comes back to ships for the Vikings. Walls were made of thick timbers sunk into the ground with planks or wattle, with daub in between—no windows. The thatched roof rested on wooden beams. Often the building was divided in half, with stalls for livestock at one end and the family's living area at the other.

+ HOME TURF +

Later in the Viking Age, after about 870, settlers made it to Iceland and Greenland, where trees were small and scarce. Their homes were built of turf, cut and stacked like bricks to build walls and laid over driftwood beams for the roof so that grass grew on top of the houses. Sometimes the foundations were dug into the ground for insulation. The overall concept is similar to the turf houses their descendants would later build on homesteads in the American Midwest.

MODERN VIKINGS

You don't have to sacrifice comfort or air quality to enjoy the best aspects of Viking homes. A roaring fire is a good place to start. If you have exposed beams, you're halfway there. Instead of individual chairs around a formal dining table, go for rustic wooden benches with a dark finish. Try mixing textures: on a dark leather sofa, layer nubbly woolen blankets and faux-fur pillows, with a sheepskin rug where your faithful hound or half-wild cat can curl up in front of the fire. Keep some dice on your wooden chest coffee table, prepared for a friendly wager, and always have your drinking horns polished and ready. Regular wax candles are fine to set the mood—you might find that far fewer people take you up on your famous Viking hospitality if you insist on burning authentic fish oil for light.

Home Decor

Inside, the only light came from hazy fish oil (pleasant, I know) or tallow lamps, smoky central and cooking fires, and the hole in the roof that all the smoke was supposed to escape through. Can't imagine it was super effective.

Built-in benches along the walls served as seating, storage, and beds, with long, narrow wooden tables. Needless to say, privacy was hard to come by, although the husband and wife might have a closet bed with shutters that closed. Wealthy royals occasionally had large, decorated wooden beds. Most people slept under heavy woolen blankets and possibly down comforters. For additional storage, wooden chests and boxes came in handy, some elaborately carved and some with clever iron locks. The lady of the house kept all the keys on a ring on her belt as a symbol of her status.

VIKING FAMILIES

All in the Family

A Viking household was made up of a married couple and their children, with servants for wealthy families. Vikings, like other groups in the Viking Age and Middle Ages, might have anywhere from no children to ten or even twelve—and, oh yeah, no separate bedrooms. Can you imagine?

Childhood in the Viking Age was mostly an apprenticeship for adulthood. Archaeologists have found children's toys, including dolls, ships, swords, and small animal figures. But many toys could also work as teaching tools for adult tasks: a

A child's toy, or basically a Viking-era My Little Pony

spinning top might teach a child the motions of spinning wool into thread, and a wooden sword could be used for training.

Vikings mostly educated their children by having them help with chores and grooming them to perform adult tasks. Children might tend the fire or gather firewood, help with cooking, pick berries, or take care of animals. In the poem "RigsÞula," a myth about the creation of the social classes, only the upper-class children of the nobleman named Jarl learn to read and write runes.

Coming of Age

Life was hard in the Viking Age, with a high infant mortality rate and women at great risk of dying in childbirth. If parents could not afford to support a new child, infanticide, or leaving a baby out to die, was legal into the 1200s. With life expectancy hovering around a mere forty to forty-five years, children who survived grew up quickly. Boys could inherit at age sixteen, and girls could marry as young as twelve. They were considered adults as soon as they were married.

+ THE CAT'S PAJAMAS +

If you're wondering whether the Vikings were an animal-loving bunch, I can report that they mostly used cats and dogs as working animals. The Vikings kept cats to catch mice—but these were no ordinary domestic cats. Scandinavian cats were domesticated from the wild *skogkatt*, or Norwegian forest cat, which was big boned with a large ruff and lynx-like tufts at the tips of the ears. New brides often received kittens as gifts to help them set up a mouse-free new home—it was especially appropriate because cats were a symbol of Freyja, the goddess of love.

+ A DOG'S LIFE +

Canine companions had to work like dogs—Vikings kept them for hunting and herding. But they weren't just working animals. Many rune stones include carvings of dogs accompanying their masters to the afterlife, and Viking graves often contain the bones of dogs sacrificed at the funeral. If it sounds barbaric, remember we're talking about Vikings—it's actually rather sweet (in a twisted way) that these chieftains couldn't imagine going to Valhalla without their loyal hounds.

THE LOOK FOR MEN

You may imagine Vikings outfitted in nothing but fur and leather, but archaeological evidence shows that most clothing was made of woven wool and linen fabric, with silk trim on fancier pieces.

• TROUSERS: Vikings wore a couple of different styles: narrow, tailored leggings and baggy knee-length pants. Men wore leg wrappings, or puttees, in a variety of colors with trousers of both styles. Narrow strips of cloth were wound around the calves, covering the hems of the pants and offering extra warmth and protection against wear and tear.

- **TUNICS**: These long-sleeved shirts reached below the waist and could be layered for warmth. Usually made of wool, tunics could have a rounded neckline or a keyhole collar with a single button or bead to hold it shut. Some were cut close to the body, while others used extra cloth to create a flared waist. They might feature trim or embroidery at the neck and cuffs.

- **CLOAKS**: Men pinned their cloaks with a metal brooch at the shoulder to keep their sword arms free—so you could tell at a glance whether a man was right or left handed. Cloaks were made from a single rectangular piece of fabric, ranging from lightweight woven wool to thick, shaggy wool thought to be a type of faux fur. The graves of some high-ranking individuals contained fur-lined cloaks with colorful silk trim or plaid cloaks with fringe.

- **COATS**: Some men in the eastern Swedish city of Birka wore long Rus riding coats, buttoned from neck to waist and open below. Historians believe they were adapted from the Byzantine Empire's long coat called a *skaramangion*. Trade with Russia was well established at the beginning of the Viking Age, and the Vikings imported fashions as well.

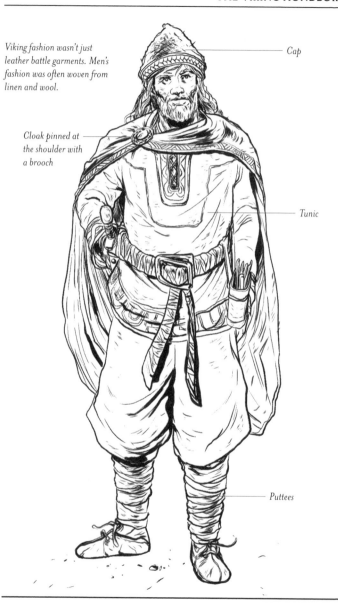

Viking fashion wasn't just leather battle garments. Men's fashion was often woven from linen and wool.

Cap

Cloak pinned at the shoulder with a brooch

Tunic

Puttees

- **CAPS**: Men's caps were made from leather or woven fabric and had either rounded or pointed tops. Rich men might have embroidered or woven trim—and among the fashionable set in Birka, metal knot work seems to have been popular. Men wore helmets in battle (but not with horns!)—see Horned Helmets on page 115 for details.

- **BELTS**: Simple metal buckles have been found in many graves, with traces of both leather belts and colorful tablet-woven fabric belts. A man might carry a knife on his belt alongside a purse containing a comb, a nail cleaner, flint, gaming pieces, or coins.

- **SHOES AND BOOTS**: Men and women both wore leather shoes and short boots, either slip-ons, laced, or buttoned. They were generally plain—Vikings didn't risk sewing precious silk or woven trim to the hems of their skirts or trousers, let alone waste it on footwear.

+ ALL-WEATHER GEAR +

Since Northern Europe is not known for its sunny climate, Vikings developed a method of making moisture-shielding outerwear. They rubbed skins with beeswax to soften the leather and treated them with fish oil for waterproofing.

THE LOOK FOR WOMEN

Even rich Viking women lived active, outdoorsy lives, and the layered look was a practical solution that also offered plenty of opportunities for decoration. As with men, fur and leather played a much smaller role with women than pop culture leads us to believe. Working our way outward, here's a breakdown of the four main layers:

- **SHIFT**: The innermost garment would be floor length with long sleeves, made of woven, undyed linen. Regional variations included a boatneck versus a keyhole neckline closed with a small metal brooch, pleats versus smooth, and gores added for fullness (à la homemade bell-bottoms) versus straight cut. In Birka, it was fashionable to wear a pleated shift and let your slip show under a shorter gown.

- **GOWN**: Also floor length with long sleeves, this tunic went over the shift and could be linen or wool. It was usually dyed bright colors, with the sleeves and torso embellished with embroidery, braid, or appliquéd strips of imported silk. The fancy Swedes of Birka, which was a market town, sometimes used metal trimmings like knotted strips of silver wire or looped metal meshwork. A few areas used fur trimmings, but not many groups treated fur as a decoration.

Viking women wore woven gowns and caftans, with plenty of decorative embellishments.

Caftan pinned with a brooch

Gown

Shift

- **APRON DRESS**: This wraparound piece had shoulder straps rather than sleeves, pinned in place by distinctive oval brooches. The cloth was less heavily decorated, as you might expect for an outer garment that saw a lot of wear and tear.

- **LONG COAT OR CAFTAN**: No, not a 1970s Elizabeth Taylor–style caftan, although that would be awesome. This was a floor-length, long-sleeved wool coat that pinned shut with another large brooch at the chest. Like the gown, the sleeves and bodice of the caftan were heavily embellished and might have been lined with linen or silk. It replaced the more shapeless shawl and went out of fashion later in the Viking Age as pleated shifts became more popular.

Local Color

Homegrown ingredients like the root of the madder plant and the leaves of yellow flowering woad dictated many of the colors in a Viking woman's wardrobe.

- **BLUE**: Scandinavia
- **DARK RED**: The Danelaw in England
- **PURPLE**: Ireland

For more on dyeing techniques, see Weaving and Sewing, page 38.

MODERN VIKINGS

Add a little Viking flair to your look. Natural linen and wool are great choices, as are longer skirts (pleated midi skirts are having a moment as of this writing). Try a long wool cardigan, leather boots with pointed toes, and a coat with a fur-trimmed hood. Check the fabric store for ribbon with a diagonal geometric pattern on a bright background for a trim that approximates Viking Age tablet weaving. Appliqué the trim a couple of inches above the hem of a skirt or the cuffs of a shirt or sweater. Even just adding an ornate metal brooch will give you a Norse look. Most Viking women's brooches were oval or round and made of pewter or silver, decorated with fine filigree wire or interwoven animal shapes.

FARMING THE FJORDS AND FJELLS

Most farms focused on livestock: cows, sheep, horses, pigs, and some poultry. Farmers valued their animals for milk, wool, and work (plowing and riding) more than for meat—in fact, many poorer farmers would only kill and eat an animal as a last resort when facing starvation.

+ THE SUMMER SETER +

In Norway, with its steep mountainsides and scarcity of fertile land, a summer custom developed in the Viking Age of sending cows, goats, and sheep to mountain pastures called *seter*. A milkmaid and a cowherd, usually the farmer's children, stayed all summer in a simple cabin that combined a living area and a dairy. This freed up the home fields for grain or hay crops during the brief growing season. The thousand-year-old tradition has nearly died out today, as more *seter* have been converted into tourist attractions or vacation homes.

Pork became more popular with richer farmers over the course of the Viking Age, as they converted more fields from grazing land to grain crops. Pigs can forage in the woods and eat kitchen scraps, which means they need much less pasture space.

Women and men both tended animals, but the outdoor work of plowing, planting, fertilizing, harvesting, and threshing fell to men. Since "fertilizing" meant spreading human and animal dung over the whole field, the women were probably glad to let them have it.

Put Your Back Into It

As grain fields spread, barley grew best in the cold, harsh northern climate, though rye, spelt, oats, and flax also grew in some areas. Farmers used a primitive plow called an ard, which was

It's ard work: an ard was a plow-like tool used by Viking farmers.

just a wooden spike that scratched a furrow in the soil rather than turning it like a plow with a moldboard. They often had to cross-plow a field to break up the earth enough for planting. That wooden ard had to be replaced every other day as it wore down—talk about labor intensive. Toward the end of the Viking Age, iron ards saved farmers some work, and more advanced plows with moldboards reached Denmark.

A successful walrus hunt could provide a Viking village with meat and ivory, as well as ship ropes made from the hide.

HUNTING AND FISHING

Going on a Bear Hunt

The great forests in Norway, Sweden, and Denmark swarmed with game. The Vikings hunted deer, elk, wild boars, and bears with bow and arrow and with spears. We know from

written sources that Scandinavians used traps for small game like hares, although archaeological evidence is slim. In the north, hunters went after reindeer, whales, seals, and walruses. A walrus was a real prize: the meat was good, and strips of walrus skin made excellent ship ropes. Walrus-ivory tusks fetched a high price in European markets and became a major export for Greenlanders. Hunters also traded in furs from bears and otters.

Casting a Wide Net

Nets, hooks, floats, and sinkers from archaeological finds show the specialized nature of fishing equipment and its importance in the Viking Age. Large towns like Hedeby, Birka, and Jorvik seem to have relied on fish, including cod, haddock, herring, and, everyone's favorite, eels, to feed the dense population.

Fowl Weather

The steep coastal cliffs in northern Norway, the North Sea islands, and Iceland are still home to large populations of seabirds, which the Vikings trapped and ate. I suppose if you're eating a lot of fish anyway, it might not matter that the birds taste like fish too.

Recent trapping techniques in the Faeroe Islands give us a window into what a Viking bird hunt might have looked like. A team of fowlers climb the landward side of the cliffs and look over the edge toward the sea, spying birds nesting on the knife-edge outcroppings below. The hunting party uses ropes to lower one brave man, who swipes at the nesting birds with his hands and a long-handled net. They used the same technique to gather feathers and down from the nests—seems like a lot of risk just for nicer pillows.

EAT LIKE A JARL

Daily Bread

Most bread was made from barley, the main grain crop in Scandinavia. The second ingredient was grit from the stone hand mills used to grind grain. No wonder Vikings' teeth wore down so quickly. One analysis of ancient bread found in Sweden discovered that it was made up of dried peas and pine bark—the poor man's Wonder Bread. Other grains, like rye, spelt, oats, and flax, might have been added to the bread or used along with barley to make porridge. Only the rich could afford wheat.

A delicious Viking-era dried pea and pine bark loaf might have paired nicely with cheese.

Unleavened bread dough was kneaded in wooden troughs and baked in embers on long-handled iron pans. Women baked fresh bread every day, since it had to be eaten right away before it cooled off and got rock hard.

Cheeseheads

Scandinavians kept cows, sheep, and goats for their milk as well as to supply meat for special occasions. They drank the milk fresh or preserved it as sour milk for sea voyages. Women also made butter and cheese, using sieves to separate the whey for pickling.

MODERN VIKINGS

Skyr: it's the new Greek yogurt! In the past few years, the high-protein Icelandic superfood has skyrocketed in popularity in the United States, with Nordic brands competing via the authenticity of their thousand-year-old yogurt cultures. It's made from whey, after the butterfat has been removed, and strained repeatedly to yield a thick, creamy yogurt. Of course, if all you're really after is Viking-warrior levels of protein, you can look for dried codfish snacks, which boast that they're 95 percent protein.

Well Done

Meat and fish could be grilled over the fire on large metal forks and spits or boiled in cauldrons hung from chains over the fireplace. Stews would have included the most common Scandinavian vegetables: cabbage, peas, and onions. Viking Age cauldrons were made of hammered iron or copper or carved from soapstone. Soapstone is soft enough to shape with a knife and retains heat for a long time, which makes it ideal for cooking. Ladles and strainers were made of wood.

Viking meals were cooked in cauldrons suspended over a fire.

To prepare for winter, women had a variety of options for preserving meat and fish. They could salt it with salt obtained by boiling seawater. They could also pickle it in brine or in whey, a byproduct of cheese making. In some regions, the Vikings may also have used smokehouses.

+ THROWING CODFISH TO THE WIND +

Fishermen on the Lofoten Islands have been wind drying fish and fish heads on wooden racks for thousands of years, and they're still at it. The fish are hung to dry in January and February, and the fillets are ready for export by April or May. The strings of fish heads, hung up like ropes of garlic, provide photo ops for tourists into July, when loaders and backhoes take a break from road construction to scoop up the heads. Today, they're mostly ground up for fish meal and sold around the world as far as sub-Saharan Africa.

Table Manners

Carving boards for meat have been found at archaeological sites, and ordinary axes were used for butchering animals and cutting up meat. Wooden troughs and trays with finely carved handles appear in wealthy graves and must have been used for serving food.

Time to set the table: Viking era utensils, plus an axe, just in case.

Plates were usually simple wooden disks, while bowls could be made of clay or soapstone. Every man, woman, and child had their own knife and a spoon made of wood or polished horn, but mostly the Vikings ate with their fingers. My kind of people.

A VIKING BREW

The Brewmistress at Work

Most Viking farms had their own brewing setup run by the lady of the house, and the whole family drank beer every day (safer than water!). Luckily, the staple grain in Scandinavia, barley, tastes much better in beer than in bread. A full break-down of home brewing is way beyond the ambitions of this book, but let's talk about Viking processes and ingredients.

+ **MALT**: Malted barley is the base for beer, with yeast added for fermentation and herbs for flavor. Women would malt the barley by soaking the grains and allowing them to germinate or sprout, then drying and toasting them.

+ **YEAST**: Europeans in the Viking Age didn't know what yeast was or how it worked—Louis Pasteur discovered its secrets in 1859. Rather, they viewed fermentation as a gift from the gods. The Norwegian name for "the thing that brings the ale into being" was *bryggjeman*, brewing man, or the spirit of the ale. Each family did have its own accidental heirloom strain of yeast, though, preserved on stir sticks passed

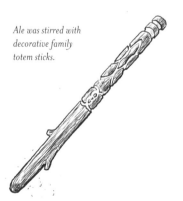

Ale was stirred with decorative family totem sticks.

down through generations. These totem sticks might be carved or decorated to celebrate their powers. Talk about a magic wand: wave it over barley stew and watch it turn into beer!

- **HERBS**: Hop heads, get your noses out of the Cascadia and look around your yards! There's so much more to Viking brewing than quibbling over Citra versus Simcoe. Here are some plants the Vikings could have mixed and matched.

Herbs like bog myrtle, wormwood, and mugwort added unique flavors to ale.

+ *Yarrow*: A widely used medicinal herb and one of the most common additions to beer, as you might guess from its Scandinavian names: *ølkall* (ale man), *jordhumle* (earth hops), *skogshumle* (forest hops), *gjede-brygger* in Denmark (goat brewer), and *vallhumall* in Iceland (meadow hops).

+ *Wormwood*: Yes, the main ingredient in absinthe. It gives a very bitter flavor, so use just a pinch.

+ *Mugwort*: Less bitter than wormwood, and sounds even more like something out of Harry Potter.

+ *Bog Myrtle:* The strong flavor is matched by strong effects: use sparingly or expect a hangover.

+ *Saint John's Wort:* Also has a strong effect and was used more for flavoring spirits after the Middle Ages, when the art of distilling came to Scandinavia.

+ *Pine and Spruce Resin:* In the Finnish epic poem *Kalevala*, the brewer starts the ferment of the wedding ale by adding spruce cones and pine twigs. Plenty of modern breweries are experimenting with spruce-tip ales.

+ *Heather:* This purple-flowered shrub grows especially well in Scotland, so Viking settlers on the Orkney and Shetland Islands might have used it most. Like bog myrtle, it's highly intoxicating. It also sometimes grows a piggybacking moss variety that the Scots call the fogg, which might take your beer from magic yeast to magic mushrooms.

+ *Dandelion:* Try it; you might like it—or at least you can get it for free. Leaves and stems both work.

+ *Juniper:* A popular bittering agent that works well alongside hops. It's also the main flavoring herb in gin.

+ *Hops:* Hops have been found in the ruins of the Danish market town Hedeby, although they came late to Norwegian brewing, after the Viking Age.

MODERN VIKINGS

The Norwegian farmhouse yeast strain known as *kveik* is seeing a resurgence in the brewing world. The Norwegian writer Lars Marius Garshol has done a lot of the legwork to analyze what sets Norwegian farm brewing apart, digging up traditions that date back hundreds of years (if not all the way to the Viking Age). His blog is the perfect rabbit hole for home brewers, with detailed descriptions of brewing alongside wise old mountain men over open fires in massive stone hearths. Visit the legendary Larsblog at www.garshol.priv.no for more.

Some *kveik* beers to watch for:

BREWERY	BEER
Alvarado Street Brewery	Logical Step
Stone Brewing	Hi, I'm Kveik
Tombstone Brewing	Norwegian Farmhouse IPA
Hacienda Beer Co.	Rano Pano
Shades of Pale Brewing	*Kveik* series of special releases

HONEY AND MEAD: NECTAR OF THE GODS

Mead, a type of honey wine, had deep significance for the Vikings. Where beer was an everyday drink, they broke out mead for special occasions. In the poem "Hávamál," Odin, the father of the gods, tells how he sneaked into the mountain hall of a giant and seduced his daughter into letting him drink the mead of inspiration. He brought it back to the rest of the gods, giving the world the gift of poetry. We think it's pretty badass to be the god of battle, mead, *and* poetry all at the same time.

LITTLE IS LACKING TO THE WISE,
FOR THE SOUL-STIRRER NOW,
SWEET MEAD OF SONG,
IS BROUGHT TO MEN'S EARTHLY ABODE.

—HÁVAMÁL

Hive Mind

To make mead, you need honey. To get honey, you need bees. By the Viking Age, people no longer had to cross their fingers they'd stumble upon a wild beehive in the woods. The

Skeps, basket-like beehives, were one of the earliest types of artificial hives for domesticated bees.

earliest evidence of domesticated beehives in the Viking world comes from the Norse colony of Jorvik in northern England, present-day York. They made basketlike hives known as skeps out of coils of straw one or two feet high, giving them that iconic dome beehive shape.

Viking beekeepers would cut out the honeycombs and place them in a cloth bag to drain premium clear honey. Wringing out the bag with the comb inside produced B-grade honey. Then they would take the bag, leftover honeycombs, and scraps of wax and soak the whole mess in warm water to dissolve any remaining honey. Strain this bee-trash soup, and what's left is the base for mead.

The fermentation process is actually very similar for mead and beer: stir with the magical yeast-bearing stick, let it activate, and finish with herbs for flavor. The result is a semidry to sweet honey-flavored wine, higher in alcohol than most beers. Mead can be mixed with beer or brewed with malted barley, like beer, to create the even stronger dark-brown concoction known as braggot. The adventurous souls at Dogfish Head Craft Brewery have created a few different braggot releases in recent years.

+ WINE AMONG THE BARBARIANS +

As Ernest Hemingway wrote, "Wine is one of the most civilized things in the world"—which could be why the Vikings never learned to make it. Almost no wine grapes grew in Scandinavia, yet the Vikings did occasionally make fruit wines, which were probably the strongest alcoholic beverage they knew. Instead, wine was imported from the Rhine River regions in Germany via the North Sea ports of Hedeby and Dorestad; thanks to its cost and rarity, only the upper classes could afford to drink it. Viking raids also swept along rivers in France, attacking famous wine regions like Bordeaux and the Loire valley. Actually, as soon as we finish writing this book, we're going to run out and start a "Plunder and Pinot" wine-tasting tour to retrace their routes.

WEAVING AND SEWING

Weave Your Magic

Viking women all participated in making clothes for their families, and it's possible that some women in cities and towns specialized in textile production, running their own businesses. Starting with clumps of raw wool, women combed it smooth and spun it into fine thread on a distaff or hand spindle. Vikings also made linen thread from the stalks of the flax plant.

Next, the women set aside some of the thread to be dyed. Linen does not take dyes as easily as wool, so many linen pieces would have been left their natural color or dyed with a stronger dye like blue woad, made from the leaves of a plant in the cabbage family (the same dye that William Wallace of *Braveheart* fame used as face paint). We have evidence of a wide variety of local plants used to create different colors:

- **RED**: Madder root or bedstraw
- **YELLOW**: Still unknown; testing has eliminated twenty-five possible sources, including saffron and chamomile
- **GREEN**: Unknown yellow and woad
- **BLUE**: Woad

- **PURPLE**: Lichen, sometimes mixed with madder for a reddish-violet tone
- **BROWN**: Walnut shells, sometimes with iron added to darken the color

With a palette of different-colored threads at the ready, weaving could begin. The most common weaving setup was a warp-weighted loom. For a quick (and bloodthirsty) tutorial on weaving, we turn to *Njál's Saga*:

Inside, he could see women with a loom set up before them. Men's heads were used in place of weights, and men's intestines for the weft and warp; a sword served as the beater, and the shuttle was an arrow. And these were the verses they were chanting:

> *Blood rains*
> *From the cloudy web*
> *On the broad loom*
> *Of slaughter.*
> *The web of man,*
> *Grey as armour,*
> *Is now being woven;*
> *The Valkyries*
> *Will cross it*
> *With a crimson weft.*

The warp is made
Of human entrails;
Human heads
Are used as weights;
The heddle-rods
Are blood-wet spears;
The shafts are iron-bound,
And arrows are the shuttles.
With swords we will weave
This web of battle.

If you can look past the gory war imagery, you can see that a team of women worked together on a vertical loom held taut by weights, occasionally inserting new colored threads by hand (the Valkyries' "crimson weft") to create elaborate patterns. The cloth might be used for tapestries, sails, blankets, or clothing. We don't know how or if Vikings used patterns, but they did piece together cut fabric to create complex garments like tailored trousers, tunics with inset sleeves, and dresses and tunics with added gores for fullness.

See The Look for Men on page 12 for more details about men's clothing, and the Look for Women on page 16 for women's.

All the Trimmings

Another ancient form of weaving, tablet weaving, was used to create decorative braid and trim. This method predates the Vikings and was used across Europe. Instead of using a loom, a weaver would slip a warp thread through each hole in a thin wooden tablet, repeating until she had a stack of tablets. Turning the tablets as the shuttle weaves through the warp threads creates a wide variety of patterns. Vikings often used metallic thread spun from thin silver wire, sometimes gold.

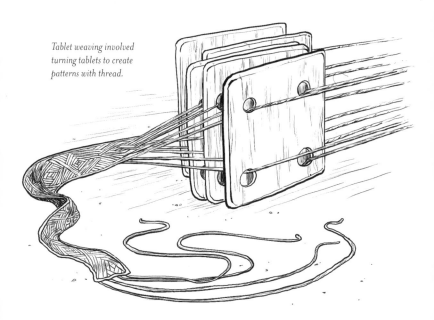

Tablet weaving involved turning tablets to create patterns with thread.

Embroidery, while not common among Vikings, appears in scattered tenth-century archaeological sites in Sweden, Norway, Denmark, and the Viking-dominated city of York in England. The stitches we can identify include stem, chain, herringbone, split, and couching.

Not a Knit

The Vikings didn't knit—they used an earlier technique called naalebinding. This is a looped single-needle stitch analogous to crochet, with a few main differences. The naalebinder uses

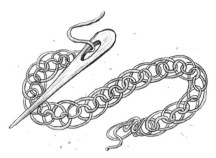

Vikings used naalebinding to create socks, caps, and mittens.

a short length of working yarn (rather than a whole ball of yarn) to create interlocking loops, pulling the full length of the yarn through the loop each time. When the yarn runs out, another piece is spliced onto the end. Unlike knitting, naalebinding doesn't unravel; finishing a piece is as easy as threading the end of the yarn back through the last few loops. Vikings used naalebinding for socks, caps, and mittens. When knitting was introduced to Europe sometime in the thirteenth century, by Middle Eastern Muslims living in Spain, it turned out to be faster than naalebinding and quickly overshadowed the older technique. Literally anything is faster than tying thousands of knots in one long piece of string.

THE VIKING TOOL CHEST

The Practical Blacksmith

Most farms handled their own ironwork, making everything from weapons to cooking implements to nails, in a setup that would have resembled a common medieval smithy centuries later. An assistant kept the charcoal fire hot with the bellows, while the blacksmith used tongs to move red-hot iron from the hearth to the anvil, where he hammered it into shape. Specialists sometimes worked with sheet metal, using shears to make precision cuts. Archaeologists have found small cauldrons hammered in one piece and larger cauldrons made from several thin sheets cut out and riveted together. Soapstone cauldrons are much more common, however—the soft stone was less expensive to shape than iron. Some smiths who worked with precious metals had crucibles for melting bronze or silver, as well as drawplates for drawing wire to create filigree.

One thing Viking blacksmiths didn't make was horseshoes: only wealthier Vikings owned horses, so most blacksmiths didn't cater to them. Even when horses became more common in the 900s, horseshoes didn't become widespread in Scandinavia until after the Viking Age, between 1100 and 1300.

Woodworking

The most important tool for a woodworker was a good axe. With just the axe, he could cut posts and planks for houses, furniture, and ships and hew rough outlines of tool handles and plows before finishing and shaping with a knife. The Swedish expression *"yxa till"* (make with an axe) still means to rough something out or create a prototype.

From left to right, an axe, adze, and auger were tools used by Viking woodworkers.

The main tools for shaping wood were adzes and knives, with augers for boring holes, and a variety of chisel types. Two-handled drawknives for smoothing and shaping wood and scalloped molding irons for gouging decorative shapes (think crown molding) were both used for larger pieces, especially ships. See Boatbuilding on page 88 for more information on shipbuilding.

+ THE MÄSTERMYR HANDYMAN +

A well-equipped tool chest found in a bog at Mästermyr, on the Swedish island of Gotland, gives us a clear picture of a traveling handyman of the late Viking Age. The hundred-plus tools inside included woodworking and ironworking implements as well as a few tools of the coppersmith's trade. The "Mästermyr man" had hammers of various sizes, files, rasps, shears and tongs for working sheet metal, punches for decorative metalwork, lock parts and keys, augers, gouges, drawknives and adzes for shaping wood, and of course a few axes. It's rare to find Viking-era saws, but he had one each for wood and metal.

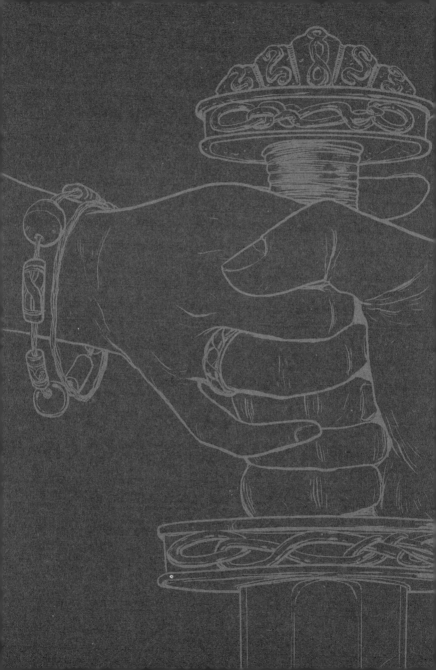

THE
KINGDOM

SOCIAL
LIFE

FEASTS AND FESTIVALS

Party Like It's 999

The Viking Age was born in the great halls of chieftains who built friendships and alliances through generous feasts and gift giving. Large parties set the stage for distributing last summer's loot from raiding and recruiting for next summer. Hospitality was huge with the Vikings in general, as we can see in the sagas of kings and gods, and the god Odin's sayings in the "Hávamál":

> Hast thou a friend whom thou
> trustest well,
> from whom thou cravest good?
> Share thy mind with him,
> gifts exchange with him,
> fare to find him oft.

Not ones to pass up the chance for a great feast, Vikings held many celebrations. Cheers, or skål, as the Scandinavians would say today.

Vikings offered round after round of toasts or *fulls* at feasts, for victory from the gods and the king's success. They might make the sign of the hammer over the cup to honor Thor, god of thunder. Odin, father of the gods and god of battle, was said to have sworn never to drink until his friend Loki was served, so Vikings had a habit of, after every toast to Odin, flicking a few drops of their drinks into the fire for Loki—the ninth-century version of pouring one out for your homie.

'Tis the Season

Three major religious festivals stood out during the year for their emphasis on gathering and feasting: Winternights, after the harvest; Yule, in midwinter; and Midsummer. At the end of the Viking Age, the early Norwegian law code Gulaðing made it a legal requirement to brew beer for these fests, and it set the dates to match the Christian holiday equivalents: All Saints' Day, Christmas, and the feast of Saint John the Baptist.

MODERN VIKINGS

Even if you don't currently celebrate the feast of Saint John the Baptist, you can still take a hint from the Vikings and throw seasonal ale feasts in your own great hall. Try a Viking-style Oktoberfest, a midwinter Yule bonfire in December, or a summer solstice picnic. Expectant parents, assign Grandma baby-shower-planning duties, but tell Grandpa you want a *barnöl* when you bring the baby home from the hospital. You'll have leftovers for days (and sleepless nights).

Some everyday community celebrations are so identified with beer that it's part of the name: *gravöl* (a wake or "grave ale"), *barnöl* ("child ale" to celebrate a birth), and *taklagsöl* (a barn raising or "roofing ale").

GROOMING

Clean Up Your Act

If you're used to thinking of Vikings as hairy barbarians, it might surprise you to learn that Vikings were some of the most well-groomed people in Europe. And they cleaned up

*Vikings cleaned up nice: a personal groom-
ing set might have included tweezers, a nail
cleaner, and an ear spoon.*

even more for feasts and special occasions: as the ancient poem
"Hávamál" puts it, "Fed and washed should one ride to court."
Women often wore a decorative grooming set on a chain hanging from a brooch, including tweezers, a nail cleaner, and a
finely decorated metalwork or ivory ear spoon. For day-to-day
cleanliness, Vikings washed their hands and faces every morning and before meals.

The Old Norse word for Saturday is *laugardagr*, which means
wash day. They bathed and washed their clothes weekly—at a
time in history when an Anglo-Saxon might bathe once a year.
In fact, as one monk complained, the men of northern England
didn't stand a chance against Viking charm.

[THE DANES] CAUSED MUCH TROUBLE TO
THE NATIVES OF THE LAND; FOR THEY
WERE WONT, AFTER THE FASHION OF
THEIR COUNTRY, TO COMB THEIR HAIR
EVERY DAY, TO BATHE EVERY SATURDAY, TO
CHANGE THEIR GARMENTS OFTEN, AND SET
OFF THEIR PERSONS BY MANY FRIVOLOUS
DEVICES. IN THIS MATTER THEY LAID SIEGE
TO THE VIRTUE OF THE MARRIED WOMAN,
AND PERSUADED THE DAUGHTERS EVEN OF
THE NOBLE TO BE THEIR CONCUBINES.

—JOHN OF WALLINGFORD

Large farms usually had a heated bathhouse, with buckets of water for washing or sometimes a tub. In Iceland, where geothermal activity still makes hot springs a main attraction, Viking settlers used naturally heated water in their bathhouses. In spring and summer, Vikings bathed outdoors in streams and lakes—nothing wrong with a little skinny-dipping.

MODERN VIKINGS

The Finns have followed up steam rooms with cold plunges for thousands of years, training the body to maintain equilibrium in extreme situations. Recent research also suggests the temperature swing is heart healthy. As you're planning your next long weekend, try looking for a lakefront rental with a hot tub for a modified Finnish sauna experience: get steamed up, jump in freezing water, and rush back to the hot water. Repeat until you feel like your skin's going to fall off. Ale and mead are not advised for water-related shenanigans. (See A Viking Brew, page 29, and Honey and Mead: Nectar of the Gods, page 34, for better advice.)

BEARDS

Beard Power

Carvings found at archaeological sites show the wide variety of facial hair Vikings might have sported: long twists, pointed goatees, full mustaches with clean-shaven chins, even mustaches waxed to curve upward. It makes sense that there's no single Viking beard style. A farmer dealing with winter winds

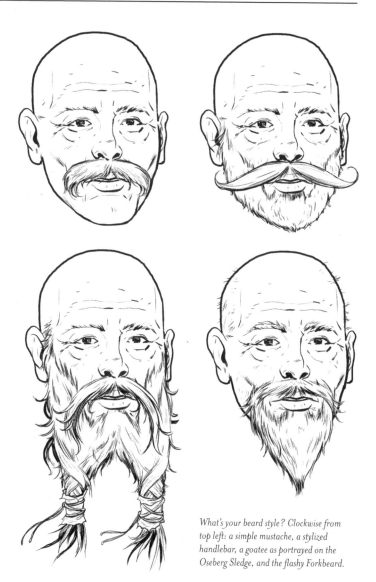

What's your beard style? Clockwise from top left: a simple mustache, a stylized handlebar, a goatee as portrayed on the Oseberg Sledge, and the flashy Forkbeard.

might grow an extremely full beard, while a warrior wouldn't want his opponents to get a handhold on his chin and so might shave more often.

Combs with fine teeth made of bone or ivory are one of the most common finds at Viking archaeological sites. Men's combs often came with special cases—the Viking equivalent of the 1950s switchblade comb. So there's no excuse for an untamed beard. A fine-tooth comb was also very useful for combating lice—sure beats shaving your head.

Heathen Haircuts

Many Anglo-Saxon men copied the hairstyles of Viking invaders and settlers, and of course the naysayers were always ready to bemoan their lack of respect. In a ninth-century letter, Ælfric of Eynsham writes to a Brother Edward, admonishing, "You reveal that you despise your kindred and your ancestors by such evil customs when you dress in insult to them in Danish fashion, with bared necks and blinded eyes." This seems to indicate a kind of reverse mullet, with the hair shaved up the back of the neck and long bangs in front. A similar cut can be seen in the Bayeux Tapestry on the Normans, who were of Danish descent.

For the perfect mix of swagger and style, nothing beats a beard braid. Try a small fishtail braid inset in a well-conditioned beard. Or follow in the footsteps of Forkbeard and try a pair of rope braids. A small bronze or pewter bead at the end adds some flair, but much more than that could push into Jack Sparrow territory.

The Viking habit of washing their faces every morning also applied to beards, especially the beards of people who get a heavy, sweaty workout every day (chopping wood and cruising on the elliptical are equal in this case). Some natural oils well known to the Vikings make great beard conditioners. A few drops of hempseed or linseed oil combed through your beard after a wash will make you presentable to even the toughest shieldmaiden.

MODERN VIKINGS

Your beard style should fit your lifestyle. Are you more of an Oseberg Sledge man, a smooth courtier type with a simple mustache? Or do you take after the fierce Sweyn Forkbeard, who invaded England four times before getting himself crowned king five weeks before his death in 1013? Now that's a beard we'd follow into battle.

WOMEN'S HAIR

Let Your Hair Down

Unmarried women often let their hair flow long and loose and sometimes wore braids. Across Scandinavia, we find an elegant fabric band called a fillet worn across the forehead like a coronet, often tablet woven with metallic threads. A veil might be pinned to the fillet to cover the hair. Married women often covered their hair, but it wasn't required. Coverings were more common in Christianized areas. Wives in Jorvik wore plain silk hoods that tied under the chin with linen straps, while Dubliners wore caps made of two squares of wool cloth sewn together, forming a point at the back of the head.

+ MAYBE SHE'S BORN WITH IT +

So you think all Swedes are naturally blond? Better make sure the *dal* (valley) matches the *fjell* (mountain). Viking men and women alike sometimes bleached their hair for a brassy blond or red tone. They used a lye-heavy soap to strip the color from dark hair.

Viking women's hairstyles often included braids. Clockwise from top left: modern-looking war braids, a fillet and veil, a cap typical of Dubliner Vikings, and silk caps worn by Jorvik women.

Carvings of women and Valkyries often show their hair tied in an elaborate pretzel knot, either coiled into a bun or with the ends flowing free below the knot. More detailed carvings show long braids arranged in a bun. Some historians believe the knot could represent a scarf tied around the head: purple fringed scarves have been found in Dublin.

War Braids

Taking the knotted style to the extreme, the History network TV show *Vikings* depicts Lagertha and other female characters wearing their hair in a Mohawk-like pile of large and small braids. It's a fierce look, well suited for warrior shieldmaidens, even if it's not fully based on archaeological evidence.

MODERN VIKINGS

Since no carving can show the full detail of a hairstyle and written descriptions of hair are hard to come by, feel free to experiment and find your own look. Try war braids for a beach bonfire, if not a full-scale reenactment. A waterfall braid offers a looser priestess style that translates equally well to a divination ceremony or a maiden's dance. Fierce Valkyrie types might look best in a crown of Dutch braids, a type of inverted French braid with a sleek, streamlined attitude.

JEWELRY

Brooches

All Vikings wore brooches to fasten their clothing, even poorer men and women, and everyone wore the most ornate version they could afford. Men's cloaks were often fastened with penannular or semicircular brooches adapted from Scottish or Irish fastenings. Women wore two domed oval brooches to secure the straps of their overdresses, and often a third, still more lavish brooch to secure a coat or shawl. Some masterful pieces in silver and gold might have been specially commissioned for wealthy families.

Viking brooches had detailed filigree designs.

Smiths achieved fine detail work with the filigree technique. First, the smith would mold the basic piece. Then, to create the filigree, he would hammer long, thin sections of the precious metal into wire. For extra-fine work, he might press the wire into a mold so it resembled a string of beads. Then the long strands were soldered to the base object in the shape of vines, braids, or animals. A smith could add further detail with granulation, a technique of soldering small metal grains to the base object.

Less well-to-do women bought rough copies of expensive oval brooches in cheaper metals, which were mass-produced with clay molds. About one thousand examples of the commonest type of this brooch have been found across the Viking world, from Iceland to Kiev. Contrary to what we might expect, the designs get cruder in later years. Experts speculate that as shawls and coats became more fashionable, the oval dress brooches were no longer meant to be seen.

Necklaces

As a tenth-century Arab traveler wrote, the Vikings would "go to any length to get hold of colored beads." Any Viking woman who could afford even a few colorful glass beads wore a strand around her neck or hanging between the two brooches fastening her overdress. Some women wore beads of silver, gold, amber, or imported crystal or carnelian. Arabian, Byzantine, and Frankish coins could be added to necklaces as well—many coins have been found with added loops to create pendants. Men occasionally wore pendants as well, with representations of the god Thor's magical hammer being especially popular.

+ SØLJE: A DEEP-ROOTED TRADITION +

The traditional *sølje* brooches that Scandinavian men and women wear today with *bunads*, or folk costumes, have their roots in Viking filigree brooches. In the 1600s, Norway was developing a silver-mining industry, and rural silversmiths, especially in central and western Norway, continued the tradition of working in filigree. They traded ideas with foreign smiths and tested new innovations, including one of the most typical features seen in *sølje* today: tiny spoon-like pendants that dangle from a filigree base.

As Norway's national identity gained strength throughout the 1800s, leading up to full independence from Sweden in 1905, *bunads* and traditional rural brooches took on an important role. Today, Scandinavians and some Scandinavian Americans wear bunads with filigree *sølje* at special occasions such as baptisms and confirmations and on national holidays like Norway's Constitution Day, known as Syttende Mai.

Gotland, an island south of Stockholm in the Baltic Sea, shared many cultural influences with the Slavs to the east that are reflected in the jewelry created and imported there. Archaeologists have discovered magnificent examples of Slavic jewelry in buried hoards of silver, including finer filigree work than Swedish smiths could execute and spheres of rock crystal set in silver pendants. Very few Vikings picked up the Slav fashion of wearing elaborate earrings—they never really took an interest in piercings.

Rings and Arm Rings

In a society that didn't use money, jewelry served as a portable wealth and status symbol. Men and women both wore solid neck rings, arm rings, and finger rings. At a wedding, a Viking bride and groom would exchange rings, just as in modern Western culture. Smiths created rings of all sizes from twisted or braided rods of silver or gold.

Examples of Viking rings, from simple circles to braided and stamped designs.

Vikings often returned from voyages to the east with sacks of silver coins—Arabic dirhams have been found buried for safekeeping in many Viking hoards. But as James Graham-Campbell writes in *The Viking World*, "What was the use of a bag full of silver coins in an economy that was not coin-using? It might be buried in the ground for safekeeping, but if the silver was only going to be weighed out when needed for some transaction, the coins might as well be melted down and turned into ornaments. These could always be cut up later if small change was needed; meanwhile they could be displayed for the prestige they would bring."

Rulers are often referred to as ring givers or ring breakers in Viking-era poetry—they gave out rings or broke up large rings to divide among warriors to reward their loyalty. This fragment of a poem written by the eleventh-century poet Arnórr is probably about King Cnut of Denmark and England and shows the cultural importance of arm rings. ("Fire of the stream" is a metaphor or kenning for gold, which is often described as watery fire.)

> *Fire of the stream was set*
> *between the wrist and shoulders of the Danes;*
> *I saw men of Scania thank*
> *him for an arm-ring.*

Generosity and gratitude were the reciprocal currency of kings and warriors. Scandinavian warriors fighting for their ruler weren't just mercenaries fighting for a paycheck—they were independent warriors who chose to fight alongside their friends. Accepting the gift of an arm ring meant they owed their loyalty as a countergift.

DRINKING CUSTOMS

Raise a Glass

The Norse often drank beer and mead from drinking horns, polished cows' horns that might be decorated with elaborately engraved metal bands. Unlike a tankard or a goblet, a horn can't be set down until it's empty, which means passing it around or downing the drink in one go. As Odin suggests in the "Hávamál," "Keep not the mead cup but drink thy measure." Either way, it's a bonding opportunity.

Everything in Moderation

The sagas are full of wild, drunken parties (for more on the sagas, see Epic Poetry, page 77), but even the Vikings knew the rage of the hangover gods—although theirs weren't made of porcelain. The poem "Hávamál" has a lot to say about drinking,

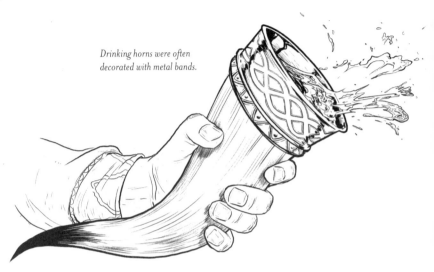

Drinking horns were often decorated with metal bands.

most of it cautionary. Probably good advice, since it's hard to imagine that Viking bar fights ever ended well.

MODERN VIKINGS

Some may consider drinking from horns a sport, but it's also an art: the shape of the horn has foiled many an unwary drinker as the first drops turn into a sudden gush. If you've put in your time to master the glass boot at Oktoberfest, you may be ready to level up to the horn. You can buy them online these days—but if you shell out for the matching stand to put your horn down between sips, we might judge you.

A BETTER BURDEN CAN NO MAN BEAR
ON THE WAY THAN HIS MOTHER WIT:
AND NO WORSE PROVISION
CAN HE CARRY WITH HIM
THAN TOO DEEP A DRAUGHT OF ALE.
LESS GOOD THAN THEY SAY
FOR THE SONS OF MEN
IS THE DRINKING OFT OF ALE:
FOR THE MORE THEY DRINK,
THE LESS CAN THEY THINK
AND KEEP A WATCH O'ER THEIR WITS.

—Hávamál

WEDDINGS

Social Contract

As in many premodern societies, Viking marriages were
arranged by the families of the bride and groom. Rather than
a religious ceremony, a Viking wedding was a social, economic,

and political contract, sealed with a handshake. Marriage often forged alliances between powerful families or ended feuds.

The bride brought a dowry to the marriage, provided by her family, and the groom contributed to it as well. This wealth remained the woman's property in the marriage, and she kept it in cases of a divorce. The groom also paid a bride-price to the bride's father or guardian. Part of the thought was that if he couldn't afford the expense of getting married, he wouldn't have the ability to support children, either, something the laws were very concerned with.

+ YOU GIVE LOVE A BAD NAME +

Roses are red, violets are blue—I'll stop you right there. The Vikings made composing love poetry illegal—punishable by banishment or death. Lonely swains didn't scrawl their poems in private diaries; poetry was most often recited. Publicly sharing a love poem about a woman inevitably started rumors that might tarnish her good family name and bring down the wrath of angry brothers on the love-struck suitor. I wonder what the Vikings would have thought of sexting . . .

The families didn't arrange a formal courtship period where the couple could get to know each other better before agreeing. However, the Icelandic sagas do record instances of a woman's family consulting her on the match before agreeing to her betrothal—and the five stories where a woman was not consulted before the marriage all end in complete disaster for the husband.

With This Ring . . .

On the morning before their wedding, both the bride and the groom would wash in the bathhouse found at every farm (although not at the same time—what would the mothers-in-law say!). The bride donned new clothes to symbolize her new role in life, with her hair left loose over her shoulders. She also wore a bridal crown, usually woven of straw and flowers. The groom would bring a family sword to the wedding, and he may also have carried a hammer symbol in honor of Thor, god of thunder.

Weddings took place outdoors, in a field or a sacred grove of trees. The bride walked to the ceremony, preceded by a young male relative carrying the sword that would be her wedding gift to the groom. An animal might be sacrificed to the gods, with blood captured in a bowl and sprinkled on the couple and guests to spread the blessing. (Don't worry; mead would probably work just as well for a modern wedding.)

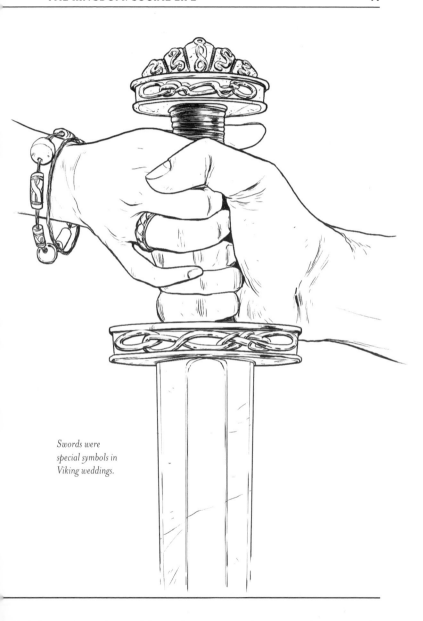

Swords were special symbols in Viking weddings.

The bride and groom then exchanged swords, a symbolic way of uniting the families. The bride's ring was offered to her on the hilt of the groom's sword, and his was given to him the same way. The symbolism of the sword both emphasized the binding nature of their vows and served as a subtle threat against breaking them. With rings on their fingers and their hands joined on the sword hilt, they said their vows.

+ RECESSIONAL RACE +

After the ceremony, rather than doing a YouTube-ready dance down the aisle, it was time for the *bruð-hlaup* or bride running, a race to the feast hall—last family there had to serve the others. This same custom can be seen in action today at most American wedding buffets.

Then it was on to the feasting, which often lasted all week. To kick things off, the bride formally served the bridal ale to her new husband, in her first duty as wife, and took her place next to him at the head table. Then an attendant brought in Thor's hammer and laid it in the bride's lap to bless the marriage and ensure fertility for the couple. The formalities extended to the end of the night, when six legal witnesses had to identify the bride and groom as they entered the bridal chamber on their wedding night.

Contingency Plans

It may come as a surprise to some, but Scandinavian women could divorce their husbands at their pleasure, unlike most other cultures at the time. Divorced women kept their dowries and could rely on their birth families to help them if the husband was slow with the alimony. Although men could have concubines among slaves or the lower classes, adultery was taken very seriously. The German monk Adam of Bremen reported that men could be executed for adultery or rape of a virgin, and women could be sold into slavery as punishment for cheating.

+ MERRY WIDOW +

In *Laxdæla Saga*, we meet the Norwegian-born widow Unn the Deep-Minded, who engineers her whole family's secret escape from Scotland after her son is murdered and who stakes an immense land claim as an early settler in Iceland. Throughout the saga, she takes charge the way a male head of household would: distributing land to her followers, freeing slaves, and arranging marriages for her grandchildren.

Widowhood offered some compensations, including retaining the wealth and property of the husband. If they wished to remarry, widows could choose their own mates without a guardian's approval.

GAMES AND SPORTS

Cross Country

The Vikings used skis for winter transportation rather than showing off their front-side 360 double shifty skills. Skiing in Scandinavia dates back thousands of years to prehistoric times, showing up on ancient rock carvings. Skiers would have had one long ski for sliding and one shorter ski for pushing off, more like an ice skate, which might be covered in leather. Arctic skis were

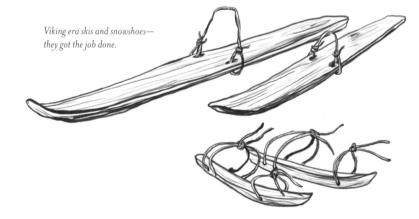

Viking era skis and snowshoes—they got the job done.

covered in leather as well, but shorter and wider than southern ski types. The modern sport evolved from military drills in the 1800s, when regional variations in skis were standardized and new innovations like the ski jump came on the scene.

Ice skates, known as ice legs, also got a practical start as winter transportation, especially in central Sweden's lake district. Vikings and their ancestors would have taken the foot bone of a horse, smoothed it flat on the underside, and bored a hole for a strap to tie it onto a shoe. Snowshoes and wooden sledges with runners also came in handy for winter travel.

MODERN VIKINGS

The wrestling style known as *glíma* came to Iceland with the first Viking settlers in the late 800s and became an official national sport in Iceland in 1906, with annual tournaments. In recent years, it's become popular in martial arts gyms, and it's naturally also a favorite with Viking reenactors. What sets *glíma* apart from Greco-Roman wrestling is not only the lack of nudity: wrestlers must remain upright, keep their grip on a belt around their opponent's waist, and stay moving. The goal is to catch the opponent off balance and throw him to the ground.

Checkmate

Long, dark nights by the fire gave rise to several types of Viking board games, including variations on checkers and the modern British game fox and geese. A chess-like game with a king called *hnefatafl* warrants several mentions in Viking poems and sagas, but the rules were forgotten when chess took over in the 1100s, at the end of the Viking Age. The archaeological evidence is fragmentary: no full game sets survive. Many warriors were buried with their gaming pieces, which would have staved off boredom and brawls on long voyages and over long winters.

Hnefatafl *pieces dot a board.*

King Sigurðr said, "I believe,
King Eysteinn, that I am stronger
and a better swimmer."
"That is true," said King Eysteinn,
"but I am more skilled and better
at board games, and that is worth
as much as your strength."

—*Morkinskinna: The Earliest Icelandic Chronicle of the Norwegian Kings* (1030–1157)

EPIC POETRY

While much of what we know about Viking history, mythology, and beliefs comes from the Icelandic sagas, most of them were actually written hundreds of years after the arrival of Christianity and the close of the Viking Age. Contemporary writings are mostly made up of skaldic poetry, singing the praises of gods, kings, and chieftains in a complex style loaded with metaphors, allusions, and complicated rhyme structures.

A skald's performance in a chieftain's great hall must have felt like a cross between a rap battle and a New York poetry reading—you'd leave impressed by the clever wordplay, and even if you weren't quite sure what the skald just said, you could be pretty sure he was bragging.

Going Platinum

The highest form of Viking poetry was the skaldic *dróttkvæt* or "court meter," poetry fit for a king's court. If writing a sonnet is like stomping an enemy mushroom in *Super Mario Bros.*, writing *dróttkvæt* is beating the big boss. Each line needs to have either an internal rhyme or assonance, with a specific pattern of alliteration.

And the more convoluted your metaphors, the better! Viking skalds used elaborate kennings: circumlocutory allusions and obscure references. For example, "the crashing of spears" is a kenning for battle. "The fire of the crashing of spears" is a double kenning for a sword. And "liquor of the rooks of the chosen of the Haddings" is an enlarged kenning for blood. Got it?

MODERN VIKINGS

While we know almost nothing about Viking music or instruments, the Vikings have inspired countless modern musicians. In 2017, a song from 1970 vaulted back into pop culture: Led Zeppelin's "Immigrant Song," arguably the most famous Viking-inspired song ever, became essentially the theme song for Marvel's superhero movie *Thor: Ragnarok*. The song stemmed from a personal connection to Iceland, as Robert Plant told a biographer: they were inspired by their tour in the land of the ice and snow.

KING AFTER KING

Building Blocks of a Nation

The Viking Age began as an era of chieftains, each controlling his own smallish territory and defending it against a constant stream of rival warlords. Power shifted constantly within small tribal regions. Through the 800s and 900s, successful chieftains or jarls began to consolidate their power and command larger and larger groups of followers, even as they kept killing each other at regular intervals. Around the year 1000, the outlines of the modern nations of Norway, Sweden, and Denmark began to take shape, though they wouldn't become politically stable for hundreds of years.

One thing that did remain stable was the need for chieftains and kings alike to earn the loyalty of their followers. Leaders relied on generosity, victory in battle, and fame and reputation to recruit warriors, in a virtuous cycle. They threw lavish feasts for their men, solidifying their friendship and loyalty by giving gifts such as gold and silver arm rings. Court poets or skalds found patrons among leaders who wanted to ensure that their victories became the stuff of legend throughout Scandinavia and beyond—the social media managers of their day.

Norway

We learn the bloody history of Viking Norway mostly from the Norwegians themselves, through skaldic poems and sagas of the kings. The first king to lay claim to a unified Norway was Harald Finehair circa 880, but his power only reached southern Norway and the fjords along the western coast. Several chieftains who were turned off by centralized power left for

NORWAY

Iceland around this time. Harald's son Erik Bloodax took over after his death around 930 but was kicked out of power for living up to his name and ruling too harshly. After decades of back-and-forth between competing Danes and Norwegians, including Harald Bluetooth (see below) and Sweyn Forkbeard, Olaf Haraldsson returned to Norway in 1015.

Fresh off the boat from many years of Viking expeditions, Olaf quickly became king over most of Norway. He imposed Christianity on the country by force, a decision that proved fatal at the time but ensured his everlasting good reputation. Olaf lost control of the north, and Cnut the Great took over. As soon as Cnut's hold weakened, Olaf came roaring back, only to lose the Battle of Stiklestad near Trondheim. Shortly afterward, Norwegian Christians came to revere him as a saint, and he remains the patron saint of Norway to this day.

Sweden

The history of Sweden is far less clear; we know the country is named after the Svear tribe from central Sweden and that the rulers of the major market town of Birka, near Stockholm, were called kings throughout the 800s. Olof Skötkonung was the first king to control both the Svear and the large Baltic Sea island of Gotland. The southern tip of Sweden, Skåne, belonged to the Danes for most of the Viking Age. In a letter to the English people in 1027, Cnut the Great boasted that he was king of "part of the Swedes," but we don't know exactly what he meant by that. What

SWEDEN

we do know is that at some point socialism took over and everyone lived happily ever after with excellent day care for all.

Denmark

The country of Denmark was probably first unified before 800, when its European neighbors began to report on its wars and politics. A comparatively orderly succession of Danish kings begins in the mid-900s with Gorm the Old. His powerful son Harald Bluetooth erected a huge compound at Jelling in the late 900s, including the two

DENMARK

largest grave mounds in Denmark and a magnificent runestone that tells us he "won for himself all of Denmark and Norway" and "made the Danes Christian." He also inspired the wireless communication standard that bears his name (with a logo made from the runes for *H* and *B*), so a thousand years after his death, he's well on his way to conquering the world.

Harald's son Sweyn Forkbeard ousted him around 987, and Sweyn's son Cnut the Great, who had meanwhile become king of England, took over around 1018 and, in a letter from 1027, called himself "Cnut, king of all England and of Denmark and of the Norwegians and of part of the Swedes." That "part of" caveat couldn't have felt good—those pesky Svear stayed just out of reach.

+ RANK AND FILE +

A snapshot of Viking ideas about class comes across in the poem "RigsÞula," or "The Lay of Rig." In the poem, the god Heimdall disguises himself as a traveler named Rig. First he comes to a poor hut, where he eats a scanty meal with a married couple and shares their bed. Nine months later the wife gives birth to a son named Thrall (slave), born to hard labor. Next, Rig stays with a hardworking middle-class couple in their house, and nine months later their son Karl (freeman) is born, an independent farmer.

Finally Rig stays in a fine hall with a well-dressed couple who serve wine and roasted birds in silver dishes, and nine months later their son Jarl (earl) is born. He learns archery, swordplay, and riding and grows up to conquer a large territory for himself. His son bears the symbolic name Kon the Younger (Kon Ungr is very close to the word *konung*, which means king) and learns to read and write runes.

This three-part account of class in Scandinavia is oversimplified, yet it does show the pervasive disdain for the lower class of thralls both in the 900s, when the poem was likely written, and continuing into the 1300s, when the earliest copy that still exists was written. There were different statuses among farmers and aristocrats, and freemen and jarls could raise their social standing by seeking fame and fortune on Viking raids.

III

THE
VIKINGS
ABROAD

SAILING TO
NEW WORLDS

BOATBUILDING

Origin Story

The Vikings traveled by ship wherever they went, whether raiding, exploring, or trading. The Viking Age exists as a milestone in history because of these ships: fast, flexible, seaworthy enough for the Atlantic but shallow enough for rivers and coastal waters. So where did they come from?

The distinctive hull of the Viking longship evolved over time in the centuries leading up to the Viking Age, but strictly as a rowing boat. The ship discovered at Sutton Hoo in Suffolk, England, can be considered a forerunner of the Viking ship. It was used for a royal burial around 625. After more than thirteen hundred years underground, all the timber had rotted away, but the distinct impression it left in the hard-packed sand revealed a clinker-built structure of overlapping planks, pointed at both ends.

It took hundreds of years for Scandinavians to start using masts and sails in their ships, which is a bit mystifying since the Romans had already introduced sailing ships to the North Sea. But once they caught on, sails sparked a maritime golden age.

Building a Viking Ship

The Scandinavians searched for ideal trees that would provide the precise shape of timber they needed for the elements of their ships. Finding these natural shapes helped give the ships their signature combination of strength and flexibility. Shipwrights seem to have preferred oak where possible, although alder, ash, beech, birch, lime, and willow were also used. Norwegians and some Swedes used pine as well.

The best source for keels and planking were oaks that grew straight upward in a dense forest, with no low branches. The keel of the Gokstad royal warship, discovered in 1880, is a single sixty-foot timber; that size of tree would be extremely rare today. Isolated oaks with broad branches stretching in different directions provided curved components like fore and aft stems and ribs. Sharply curved branches or roots provided knees for holding crossbeams and the keelson in place, similar to shelf brackets. While larger ships with higher sides had oar holes cut through the sides, smaller ships might have oarlocks shaped from a log with a projecting branch, which created a natural cradle for the oar.

An average longship, sixty-five to eighty feet long, probably required eleven midsized trees to build, plus one giant tree for the keel. Workmen felled the trees with hand axes and then split the logs radially with beech or metal wedges into wedge-shaped planks. These planks outdid sawed boards in a few different ways: they were stronger and less likely to shrink, warp, or split. They were also ideally shaped for overlapping

Many ships had ornate carvings, plus shield slots along the sides for oarmen.

clinker construction, all while being thinner and more light-weight. The bottom planks of the Gokstad ship were only one inch thick.

The shipwright would begin construction with the back-bone of the ship, attaching the fore and aft stems to the keel. Each layer of planking was fastened with iron nails, with a layer of tarred animal hair or moss in between for caulking. A master builder could see the shape emerging with each new layer and could adjust the width or the angle of the planks to create the right effect. Once the bottom hull was in place, curved ribs were added for internal support.

Next a keelson was laid on top of the keel to distribute the weight of the mast and held in place by knees. Crossbeams went in on top of the ribs, also supported by knees. Later ships included an extra layer of crossbeams and longitudinal string-ers for additional reinforcement. Many ships, especially large warships, included a signature finishing touch: a batten along the gunwale, where shields could be racked in a colorful display of strength.

The Oseberg Ship

Around the year 800, the carved picture stones on the Swedish island of Gotland began to depict ships with masts and sails. The oldest Scandinavian sailing ship yet discovered is the Oseberg ship, built around 815–820 and excavated from a grave mound in southeastern Norway in 1904. The ruins were pains-takingly reassembled and put on display in the Viking Ship Museum in Oslo, where it remains today.

This ship has been called "the finest example of artistic craftsmanship of the Viking Age," reflecting the centrality of ships to Viking culture. Both fore and aft stems feature intri-cately carved fantastic beasts, rising to spiraling snake heads. The side rails included slots where shields could be inserted for a combination of impressive visual display and added pro-tection for oarsmen. However, the mast is awkwardly attached, when compared to later ships, perhaps indicating that the ship-wright was still learning the new design.

Evolution of Ship Design

Displayed alongside the Oseberg ship in Oslo is the Gokstad ship, a slightly later design also used in a royal burial. These two ships, as the most complete specimens ever discovered, give us a good sense of Viking construction. In 1962, six ships were discovered in Roskilde fjord in Denmark that appeared to have been deliberately scuttled to barricade the fjord. They show great variation in size and shape, with more advanced ship-building techniques than the two earlier grave ships, including improved crossbeams and masts.

From these archaeological finds, combined with other more fragmentary discoveries, we can trace the evolution of ship design. Around the year 1000, shipwrights began to build specialized warships and cargo ships. Towns were getting bigger, meaning trade was growing. At the same time, the first large kingdoms developed in Scandinavia, and each official district was required to keep a ship at the ready in case of war, which naturally led to ships designed specifically for war.

MODERN VIKINGS

A reconstruction of the Oseberg ship called *Drønningen* ("the queen" in Norwegian) sank on its first trial in 1987—after just twenty seconds at sea. This led to speculation that the boat was never actually seaworthy and was a symbolic creation built specifically for the burial. In 2006, a high-tech examination of the ship revealed flaws in the original reconstruction that led to a rounder shape, shorter crossbeams, and lower sides, all of which conspired to downgrade its sailing performance. The new 2012 reconstruction, *Saga Oseberg*, crossed from Norway to Denmark successfully. While the Oseberg ship was clearly more of a royal yacht than a long-distance traveling or raiding vessel, its reputation for seaworthiness had been restored at last.

YOU USED LONG SHIPS BOLDLY,
BATTLE-STRONG LORD, AS MEN
STEERED SEVENTY VESSELS EASTWARDS.
STRAKES ROARED SOUTH, HIGH-
HOISTED SAILS CONVERSED WITH
THE FORESTAY; THE TALL-MASTED
OAK SLICED THE SOUND; *BISON*
PLUNGED ITS CURVED RAIL.

—SKALD THJODOLF ARNORSSON, IN PRAISE
OF KING MAGNUS OLAVSSON OF NORWAY
AND HIS POWERFUL WARSHIP *BISON*

The warship, or longship, was built for speed. It was comparatively slim and featured oars along its full length in addition to a mast. The shallow draft and low freeboard allowed the ship to charge right up to the beach so the warriors could run ashore through the shallows. The ships could even have carried horses: in 1970, sea trials of a replica of a Danish warship proved that horses were able to step on board over the low sides of the ship in shallow water.

Cargo ships were broader in the beam and featured a cargo hold amidships, with oars and decks for rowers positioned only at the fore and aft ends. The mast was designed to be unstepped only occasionally. Despite being designed for longer ocean travel, they were no more comfortable than the warships: both were essentially open boats. Cargo would be covered with skins, and the crew was exposed to the elements.

+ THE GOOD SHIP LOLLIPOP +

On coastal voyages, the sailors could go ashore to cook and sleep in tents. But when crossing the North Sea or sailing to Iceland or Greenland, the crew lived on dried, pickled, salted, and smoked fish and meat and hard, dry bread—a real workout for the jaw muscles. They would have to sleep where they could on deck, nestled among skin bags of water and buckets of sour milk and beer. What's that ancient Viking saying? Sour milk before beer, you're in the clear?

ON THE WATER

Sails and Rigging

The rectangular sail is one of the most distinctive features of the Viking ship in the popular imagination, and it appears on memorial runestones, coins, royal seals, and elsewhere. From these depictions, as well as written descriptions and the scanty archaeological evidence available, we see that the rigging was relatively simple and masts relatively short. Especially in warships, masts were designed to be unstepped quickly to reduce drag in unfavorable winds—which would mean the mast would need to be short enough to lay down inside the boat.

Women wove the sails from either linen or wool, sometimes in stripes or patterns, as we see in artwork of the time. To make the sails windproof and to help them last longer, they may have been treated with ochre and animal fat, as the Viking Ship Museum in Roskilde, Denmark, has done in reconstructions. Rigging could have included horsehair rope, hemp rope, and twisted walrus-hide rope.

Oars and Rudders

Oars lined the full length of warships for maximum propulsion, while appearing only fore and aft in cargo ships. The length of the oars varied according to their place on board. On smaller ships, oar pivots made of tholes, or forked pieces of wood, sat atop the gunwales. Larger ships with higher sides had oarports cut into the sides. The oarports sometimes came with small wooden disks set on a pivot that could be closed when the oars were not in use, to keep water from pouring in.

The rudder was attached to the starboard side of the stern, shaped like a broad oar and skillfully crafted. The cross section resembles an aircraft wing: the side thrust or lift created by

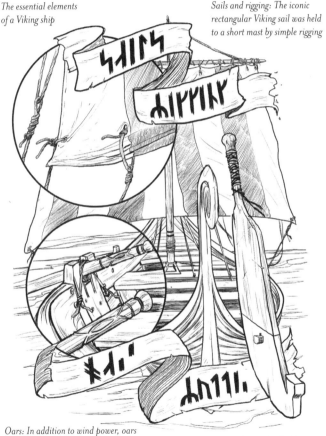

The essential elements of a Viking ship

Sails and rigging: The iconic rectangular Viking sail was held to a short mast by simple rigging

Oars: In addition to wind power, oars powered by warriors helped Viking ships speed through the water.

Rudder: Streamlined to limit resistance, the rudder helped steer.

water flowing over it compensates for the water resistance that would have otherwise pulled the ship to starboard.

+ A WORLD'S FAIR VOYAGE +

In 1893, thirteen years after the discovery of the Gokstad ship in Norway, the replica ship *Viking* was built. The Norwegian sea captain Magnus Andersen sailed across the Atlantic, and the ship appeared at the Chicago World's Fair that same year. Andersen recounted the thrill of the journey:

> *Viking did her finest lap from the 15th to the 16th of May, when she covered a distance of 223 nautical miles. It was good sailing. In the semi-darkness the light from the northern horizon cast a fantastic pale sheen on the ocean as Viking, light as a gull, glided over the wave-tops. We noted with admiration the ship's graceful movements, and with pride we noted her speed, sometimes as much as eleven knots . . . We were afforded a first class opportunity of testing Viking's performance when sailing close to the wind. To our great surprise she proved to be in the same class as most modern two-masters.*

NAVIGATION

Nature's Signposts

After generations of voyages along the coastlines of Scandinavia, Europe, and the British Isles, Viking seafarers knew the landmarks along their routes, including places to come ashore and camp at night. They would not have needed advanced navigational aids for coastal trading and raiding.

But Vikings also made frequent round trips across wide swaths of the Atlantic to Iceland and Greenland, a feat that's hard to imagine accomplishing today without a GPS, a compass, or even a map. There's no evidence of advanced navigational tools among the Vikings, so the simplest explanation is probably the best: like other premodern sailors, they were able to find their way by observing subtle signs of nature. Sailing instructions written down in the 1300s in Iceland's *Landnámabók, The Book of Settlements*, give us a sense of how a sailor would have navigated from western Norway to southern Greenland across the North Atlantic:

> From Hernar [Norway] one should keep sailing west
> to reach Hvarf, Greenland, and then you are sailing
> north of Shetland, so that it can only be seen if visibil-
> ity is very good; but south of the Faroes, so that the sea

appears half-way up their mountain slopes; but so far
south of Iceland that one only becomes aware of birds
and whales from it.

Seafarers could stay on course by visually observing some islands, while estimating the location of Iceland by knowing the habits of different seabirds and whales. Other techniques for spotting land would have included observing cloud formations, noting the reflection of ice in the sky in good weather, or even detecting the smell of sheep on the wind. They could have used the feel of the prevailing wind to estimate directions as well: warm, wet winds come from the southwest, while cold, wet winds come from the northeast.

Written accounts of traditional routes appear in the saga, along with the number of days each would take to sail. Sailors could calculate their speed by allowing for known currents, daily weather and wind conditions, and the past performance of their own ships. They may also have used a form of dead reckoning to estimate speed: tossing a floating object overboard at the bow and either counting the number of oar strokes it took to pass it or using an hourglass to time how long it took to sail past the object.

Some of the sagas also indicate that Vikings may have navigated using the position of the North Star and the sun for reference. If the sailors could keep the North Star or the sun in sight at a certain height above the horizon, checking at regular intervals, they could maintain a consistent latitude and sail directly east or west. However, this would have required clear weather for several days in a row, so it couldn't have been the only technique used.

The Myth of Sunstones

Scientists and historians have long speculated on the "solar stone" mentioned in *The Saga of King Olaf* (written after the Viking Age) and whether it could have represented a secret weapon in the Viking navigational arsenal. The saga describes the stone as being used to determine the position of the sun in overcast weather: "The king made people look out and they could nowhere see a clear sky. Then he asked Sigurður to tell where the Sun was at that time. He gave a clear assertion. Then the king made them fetch the solar stone and held it up and saw where light radiated from the stone and thus directly verified Sigurður's prediction."

Science magazine describes how a sunstone reveals the position of the sun: certain types of crystals "can split a beam of sunlight to form two images, with polarized light taking a slightly different path than the main beam. By looking at the sky through such a crystal and then rotating it so the two images are equally bright, it's possible to spot the rings of polarized light that surround the sun, even under cloudy skies." Knowing the location of the sun allows navigators to establish their own location and stay on course.

A 2018 study used a computer simulation to determine that calcite, cordierite, or tourmaline crystals could accurately guide a ship from Bergen in western Norway to Hvarf in southern Greenland. The study did not take into account weather conditions or currents that could have blown the ships off course. Of course, while it's a fascinating topic, there is still no direct evidence in archaeological or contemporary written sources that Vikings actually used crystals for navigation.

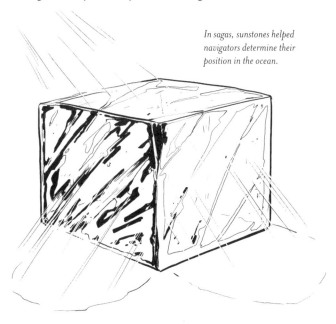

In sagas, sunstones helped navigators determine their position in the ocean.

RAIDERS AND WARRIORS

The Element of Surprise

Reports of Viking attacks often hammer home the swift, unexpected nature of the raids, describing the Norse as "rushing in," "falling upon," or "bursting in" with their ships. The unparalleled speed of their ships gave them the element of surprise in many famous battles—and also sometimes let them escape before a counterattack could even begin.

In 810, Emperor Charlemagne got word that two hundred Danish ships had attacked Frisia and extracted a large ransom from the people. The emperor, furious, led the mighty Frankish army, including an elephant given to him by a caliph of Baghdad, north to defeat them. Cue the sad trombone: the elephant died crossing the Rhine River, and soon after that, messengers told Charlemagne that the Danish fleet had turned around and gone home. The huge army never even got a chance to fight.

Spoils of War

The Vikings took every advantage they could. They exploited political divisions in the British Isles and the Frankish empire, and they didn't hold back from plundering wealthy Christian monasteries, as neighboring Christian armies might have. In fact, the starting point of the Viking Age was a raid on a monastery: Lindisfarne, in northeast England. Later, the *Anglo-Saxon Chronicle* described the attack:

> *In this year dire portents appeared over Northumbria and sorely frightened the people. They consisted of immense whirlwinds and flashes of lightning, and fiery dragons were seen flying in the air. A great famine immediately followed those signs, and a little after that in the same year, on 8 June, the ravages of heathen men miserably destroyed God's church on Lindisfarne, with plunder and slaughter.*

The wide, sandy beach on the island of Lindisfarne was a prime landing spot for the swift Viking ships. The hit-and-run approach proved so successful that the next year, another Viking crew raided a monastery just south—however, that raid ended in shipwreck and disaster. Future raids shifted west to monasteries in Scotland and Ireland.

The Vikings chose monasteries as targets not because they were anti-Christian, but because the monasteries were centers of population and wealth. They held church treasures and gifts from local nobles such as silver, gold, and fine textiles; they had large stores of food and Communion wine; and they supported large numbers of people who could be sold into slavery. Not to mention they were often poorly defended. Most historical accounts of the Vikings were written by monks and Christian scholars and naturally express bias against the "ruthless, wrathful, foreign, purely pagan people" who plundered their treasures—but they also express terror.

A haul from a monastery might have included gold, silver, and ale and wine.

Frankish Chaos

While the British Isles, and Ireland in particular, had not developed many towns and trading centers, Western Europe offered several ripe targets for the Vikings. They ravaged coastal towns between France and Poland. Their incursions up major rivers like the Elbe, Rhine, Seine, Loire, and Rhone led them to sack cities as famous as Hamburg, Paris, and Bordeaux. Important sites like these could be quickly rebuilt—which meant they could be pillaged again and again.

BITTER IS THE WIND TONIGHT
IT TOSSES THE OCEAN'S WHITE HAIR.
TONIGHT I FEAR NOT THE FIERCE
WARRIORS OF NORWAY
COURSING THE IRISH SEA.

—MARGINALIA IN AN IRISH BOOK

Defenses in the Frankish empire hit a record low in the mid-800s, and the Vikings poured through the gap left by royal infighting. After the great emperor Charlemagne died in 814,

THE NUMBER OF SHIPS GROWS: THE ENDLESS
STREAM OF VIKINGS NEVER CEASES TO
INCREASE. EVERYWHERE THE CHRISTIANS
ARE VICTIMS OF MASSACRES, BURNINGS,
PLUNDERINGS: THE VIKINGS CONQUER ALL
IN THEIR PATH, AND NO ONE RESISTS THEM:
THEY SEIZE BORDEAUX, PERIGEUX, LIMOGES,
ANGOULEME AND TOULOUSE. ANGERS,
TOURS AND ORLEANS ARE ANNIHILATED
AND AN INNUMERABLE FLEET SAILS UP
THE SEINE AND THE EVIL GROWS IN THE
WHOLE REGION. ROUEN IS LAID WASTE,
PLUNDERED AND BURNED: PARIS, BEAUVAIS
AND MEAUX TAKEN, MELUN'S STRONG
FORTRESS LEVELLED TO THE GROUND,
CHARTRES OCCUPIED, EVREUX AND BAYEUX
PLUNDERED, AND EVERY TOWN BESIEGED.

—THE MONK ERMENTARIUS OF NOIRMOUTIER

his son Louis the Pious fought openly with his three sons for
many years, crippling any attempt at a unified response to the
Northmen. The monastery on the island of Noirmoutier, a

major trading post for wine and salt at the mouth of the Loire, was raided so many times that the monks abandoned it.

The Last Viking

One of the last Viking outposts was the northern islands of Scotland, where Norse rulers held sway over territory until the 1400s. Central authorities remained weak far longer than in other areas of the British Isles, and raids continued. The last Viking standing may have been a chieftain in the Orkney Islands named Sweyn Asleifarsson, who was a successful pirate for thirty years in the late 1100s. The *Orkneyinga Saga* tells of his twice-yearly raids on the Hebrides, Wales, and Ireland, as well as attacks on English merchant ships in the Irish Sea and a monastery in the Isles of Scilly. He was finally killed in a raid on Dublin in 1171, ringing down the curtain on the Viking Age.

THE KING'S ENGLISH, OR THE VIKING'S?

Viking settlers in the British Isles left a trail of words behind that have been completely absorbed into English, like *dregs* and *keg*, *steak* and *eggs*, *gaggle* and *goslings*, *bread* and *cake*. Yale professor Roberta Frost wrote the narrative below using only "loan words"—that is, words that come from Old Norse (except conjunctions, articles such as *a* and *the*, and the verb *to be*):

> *The odd Norse loans seem an awesome window onto a gang of ungainly, rugged, angry fellows, bands of low rotten crooks winging it at the stern's wake, sly, flawed "guests" who, craving geld, flung off their byrnies, thrusting and clipping calves and scalps with clubs. But for their hundreds of kids, the same thefts, ransacking, and harsh slaughter, the wronging of husbands, the bagging and sale of thralls, the same hitting on skirts and scoring with fillies, the lifting of whoredom aloft, the scaring up and raking in of fitting gifts, seemed flat and cloying, and got to be a drag.*

The Vikings also left their mark in place-names across the British Isles, including Swansea, Fair Isle, Derby, Grimsby, Rugby, Whitby, Scunthorpe, Waterford, Wexford, and Wicklow, among hundreds more names containing *ay* or *ey*, *berg*, *by*, *dale*, *firth*, *garth*, *holm*, *kirk*, *ness*, *thorpe*, *wall*, *wick*, and many other terms.

WAR STORIES: TRUTH AND MYTHS

Did Vikings Really "Go Berserk"?

In many historical accounts, and in much of pop culture, Vikings are synonymous with ferocious violence. The medieval sagas attribute the wildest and most bloodthirsty feats to warriors sometimes called berserkers or berserks, which literally translates to bear shirts. Snorri Sturluson, one of the most famous authors of the Icelandic sagas, described berserkers as Odin's mystical warriors in his thirteenth-century poem *Ynglings Saga*:

> *Odin could make his enemies in battle blind, or deaf,*
> *or terror-struck, and their weapons so blunt that they*
> *could [do] no more but than a willow wand; on the*
> *other hand, his men rushed forwards without armour,*
> *were as mad as dogs or wolves, bit their shields, and*
> *were strong as bears or wild bulls, and killed people at*
> *a blow, but neither fire nor iron told upon themselves.*
> *These were called Berserker.*

Though berserkers may have been mythical, they inspired makers of the Lewis Chessmen, perhaps the most famous chess set in history. Found in a hoard in the Outer Hebrides, Scotland, he rook in the Lewis set pulls a classic berserker move: shiled-biting.

Historian Anders Winroth points out that most of the sagas that compared berserkers to bloodthirsty wolves, dogs, bears, and bulls were written centuries after the end of the Viking Age. The one contemporary reference to berserkers appears in a poem dedicated to King Harald Finehair in the ninth century: as the Battle of Hafrsfjord began, "bear-shirts [*berserkir*] bellowed . . . wolf-skins howled."

As mentioned elsewhere in this book, skaldic poetry contains an intricate tangle of metaphors and elaborate descriptions known as kennings. Kennings for warriors included "the tree of the sword," "feeder of ospreys," "queller of the greed of wolves," "the tree of the mail-shirt," and on and on. Winroth finds it much more likely that the bear shirts and wolf skins of the poem are descriptions of warriors in chain mail shirts.

The later medieval sagas, written after the coming of Christianity, closely associate their ideas of berserkers with long-ago pagan times. The sagas even show berserkers' powers disappearing once they accepted baptism. The most likely scenario is that the Christian saga writers spun vivid, imaginative tales of these mystical warriors to simultaneously demonize and glorify Scandinavia's pagan past.

AT THIS TIME A CERTAIN HARTHBEN, WHO
CAME FROM HÄLSINGLAND, IMAGINED IT A
GLORIOUS ACHIEVEMENT TO KIDNAP AND
RAPE PRINCESSES, AND HE USED TO KILL
ANYONE WHO HINDERED HIM IN HIS LUSTS. . . .
A DEMONICAL FRENZY SUDDENLY POSSESSED
HIM, HE FURIOUSLY BIT AND DEVOURED THE
RIM OF HIS SHIELD; HE GULPED DOWN FIERY
COALS WITHOUT A QUALM AND LET THEM
PASS DOWN INTO HIS BELLY; HE RAN THE
GAUNTLET OF CRACKLING FLAMES; AND
FINALLY WHEN HE HAD RAVED THROUGH
EVERY SORT OF MADNESS, HE TURNED HIS
SWORD WITH RAGING HAND AGAINST THE
HEARTS OF SIX OF HIS HENCHMEN [WHO HAD
CONSPIRED AGAINST HIM]. IT IS DOUBTFUL
WHETHER THIS MADNESS CAME FROM
THIRST FOR BATTLE OR NATURAL FEROCITY.

—Saxo Grammaticus, *The History of the Danes*

Lagertha in the Sky with Diamonds

Present-day Viking enthusiasts also glorify the invincible warriors they've imagined, speculating without historical evidence
that warriors might have self-induced an excess of adrenaline
to trigger the trancelike "berserker rage" of the medieval sagas,
going into a dissociative state. Others hypothesize that the
berserkers might have eaten poisonous mushrooms or grain
infected by the fungus *Claviceps purpurea*. This fungus contains
the chemical ergot, which is used to synthesize the hallucino-
genic drug lysergic acid diethylamide (LSD). All these wild
guesses originate from an unquestioned belief that a special
class of warriors called berserkers really existed in the Viking
Age, which is most likely not true.

The Vikings did understand the importance of projecting an image of ferocity, and contemporary writers among the
people they attacked recount tales of psychological warfare,
such as hanging captured soldiers in full view of their own
army to insult and terrify them. Like the Mongols did later
in history, they made the most of their bloodthirsty image in
pursuit of their real goals: wealth, fame, and political power
at home.

+ HORNED HELMETS +

While we're throwing cold water on beloved legends, we might as well take on the most pervasive one: the horned helmet. Vikings didn't wear them. Most often, they wore conical leather caps and sometimes metal helmets with rounded or pointed shapes that might have a guard for the eyes or nose.

The origins of the myth of the horned helmet can be partly explained by artwork from pre-Viking times that depicts human figures with horns. The shorter of the two golden horns, drinking vessels from circa 400, depicts naked warriors brandishing weapons, one of whom has horns on his head. The National Museum of Denmark claims these depict berserkers, who would throw off their chain mail and clothing and fight without regard for their own safety, although the golden horns predate the Viking Age by at least three centuries. Other pre-Viking figures wear helmets with horns that end in birds' heads. These were not worn in battle, where they would have gotten in the way—instead they were worn in worship of Odin, god of battle and magic, during dances and other rituals.

RAGNAR AND THE BLOOD EAGLE

Vikings on TV

The most famous Viking warrior at the moment is probably Ragnar Hairy Breeches (Loðbrók), the main character of the History network drama *Vikings*. But how much of the show is based on history? The historical advisor to the show, John Pollard, wrote that the records are slim and most of what we know was written by the people that Vikings attacked or written much later by Scandinavians who sought to glorify their own past in the sagas. "That there even was a single Ragnar is still a matter of some debate due not least to the eagerness of contemporary writers to kill him off—something which is dutifully recorded a number of times, at a number of dates and accompanied by a number of different reasons," says Pollard.

Ragnar first appears in historical accounts in 845, when he led an expedition up the Seine and sacked Paris on Easter Sunday. He and nearly all his men were said to have died in a heaven-sent epidemic on the way home.

+ DID VIKINGS HAVE NINE LIVES? +

If you're counting, the rumored deaths of Ragnar over a decade or so include the following:

1.	Died in an epidemic	France
2.	Killed in battle by other Scandinavians	Dublin, Ireland
3.	Tortured to death by other Scandinavians	Dublin, Ireland
4.	Killed by rivals	Carlingford Lough, Ireland
5.	Killed during a raid	Anglesey, Wales
6.	Thrown into a pit of venomous snakes	Northumbria, England

The Myth of the "Blood Eagle"

The legendary Ragnar Loðbrók rated his own saga, and out of the many different stories of his death, the author chose to relate how he was captured by King Ella of Northumbria and executed by being thrown into a pit of poisonous snakes. His last words refer to the wrath his sons would feel on learning of his death: "How the little pigs would grunt if they knew how the old boar suffers!" This sets up the violent revenge his sons wreak on Ella.

We know that Ragnar's sons defeated Ella in a battle in York in 866. Like their father, they had evocative but hard-to-explain nicknames: Ivar Boneless, Björn Ironside, Whiteshirt, and Sigurd Snake in the Eye. An eleventh-century poem written in honor of Ivar Boneless's descendant, the mighty King Cnut, used a typical poetic image to describe the victory: "And Ivar, he who resided in York, caused the eagle to cut Ella's back." Viking poets often used elaborate figures of speech to describe slaying one's enemies as providing food for ravens, eagles, wolves, and other carrion eaters. So Ella died in battle, and his enemies left his body out for the scavengers, a final humiliation.

But this intricate, allusive writing style known as skaldic poetry is easily misunderstood, and later readers interpreted the poem as saying "Ivar cut the eagle on the back of Ella"—which only makes sense if you really overthink it. At first, imaginative storytellers thought that Ivar had tortured Ella by carving an image of an eagle on his back while Ella was still alive.

The peak of the bloody legend comes in a fourteenth-century retelling based on the original misunderstanding: "King [Ella] was taken captive. Ivar and the brothers now recall how their father had been tortured. They now had the eagle cut in Ella's back, then all his ribs severed from the backbone with a sword, in such a way that his lungs were pulled out there." Sounds like a summer horror movie aimed at thirteen-year-old boys.

Scholars have been calling out this misinterpretation since 1984, but some historians, not to mention pop culture, are reluctant to let go of this hyperviolent spectacle.

Shieldmaidens

Circling back to the History network drama *Vikings*, we see that Ragnar's first wife, Lagertha, cuts an equally impressive figure to her husband. She fights alongside him and proves just as adept at strategy and leadership. Was she an example of an entire class of Viking women warriors?

The television character is based on stories written circa 1200 by the Danish cleric Saxo Grammaticus:

> *Ladgerda, a skilled Amazon, who, though a maiden had the courage of a man, and fought in front among the bravest with her hair loose over her shoulders. All marvelled at her matchless deeds, for her locks flying down her back betrayed that she was a woman.*

Note the references to the Greek myth of the Amazons, a society made up entirely of female warriors. Saxo was a well-educated man, and his knowledge of mythology likely bled over into his storytelling about his Scandinavian ancestors.

Excavating Our Expectations

As long as archaeologists and historians have studied the Vikings, they have concluded that Viking women had more independence and influence than women in other cultures of the era but that men still dominated society and the warrior role. In 2015, new research into a grave first excavated in the 1880s sparked widespread interest and controversy. The grave, located at the Swedish trading center of Birka (near present-day Stockholm), dates to the 900s and is one of the grandest burials of the three thousand discovered on the edge of the town. Filled with weaponry, grave goods, two horses, and one richly dressed human figure, it was clearly the grave of a high-status warrior.

The occupant of the grave was always classified as a man, but this assumption was based on the context of the grave, not close study of the skeleton. The grave contained none of the women's clothing items or domestic tools found in other females' graves. But the 2015 study, published in the *American Journal of Physical Anthropology*, proved that the bones found in that grave contained no Y chromosomes: the warrior was female.

WHAT I FIND A BIT INTERESTING IS
THAT SINCE IT WAS EXCAVATED IN
THE 1870S, IT HAS CONSTANTLY BEEN
INTERPRETED AS A WARRIOR GRAVE
BECAUSE IT LOOKS LIKE A WARRIOR
GRAVE AND IT'S PLACED BY THE
GARRISON AND BY THE HILLFORT.
NOBODY'S EVER CONTESTED IT
UNTIL THE SKELETON PROVED TO
BE FEMALE AND THEN IT WAS NOT A
VALID INTERPRETATION ANYMORE.

—CHARLOTTE HEDENSTIERNA-JONSON, COAUTHOR
OF THE 2017 AND 2019 STUDIES AND PROFESSOR OF
ARCHAEOLOGY AT UPPSALA UNIVERSITY IN SWEDEN

In the wake of viral interest in the sensational results, many
scholars questioned the science and the interpretation, saying
that the bones could have been mislabeled or a woman could
have been buried with the artifacts of a husband who died
abroad. A 2019 study by the same lead authors, published in

Skjaldmeyjar, *or shieldmaidens, lead
the souls of warriors home to Odin.*

the journal *Antiquity*, reinforced the results and methodology, rebutting the critics.

This discovery shines a light on the assumptions that can influence archaeology and anthropology, and it may lead to new research on other graves. But this single woman warrior doesn't prove that women warriors were a consistent presence on the battlefield or an accepted part of Viking society. Contemporary written sources do not mention women on the battlefield, although many poems and artworks depict fierce Valkyries leading the souls of slain warriors home to Odin. In the sagas, Valkyries are sometimes called *Skjaldmeyjar*, or shieldmaidens, but they do not fight in battles themselves.

From everything we know, we can say that Viking women could be fierce and hold respected positions, and some of them took on warrior roles, but we can't say that Viking society included an elite group of female warriors. We *can* say that we would totally watch a show about a rogue shieldmaiden fighting evil across the land . . . wait, isn't that *Xena: Warrior Princess*?

WEAPONRY

The Old Battle-Axe

No other weapon was so closely associated with the Vikings in the minds of their opponents as the axe. Axes exploded in

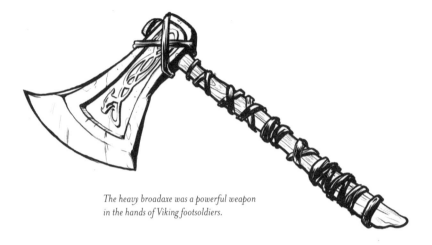

The heavy broadaxe was a powerful weapon
in the hands of Viking footsoldiers.

popularity in Scandinavia during the early Viking Age. Axes came in many varieties, but the broadaxe was most popular with warriors: they could cut through chain mail and even helmets. It took two hands to wield this formidable weapon, which made it ideal for foot soldiers and impractical for warriors on horseback. In fact, it was probably the best way to kill an enemy's horse in battle.

King Magnus of Denmark and Norway had his famous axe, Hel, commemorated in poems praising his mighty battles: "The unsluggish ruler stormed forth with broad ax . . . Hel split pallid skulls." Magnus inherited the axe from his father, King Olaf Haraldsson, who became the patron saint of Norway. So the axe Hel is the same axe that still appears on the Norwegian coat of arms.

Swords

Viking poets and scribes celebrated swords as prestige weapons, much more so than axes. The best swords came from the Frankish empire, exported as far as Russia and Baghdad. The Vikings loved Frankish swords so much that local rulers made exporting swords a crime punishable by death. Needless to say, the laws didn't stop Vikings from using the Franks' own swords against them.

Sword-making technology made great strides at the very beginning of the Viking Age. The Vikings' predecessors favored swords with elaborate gilt bronze hilts that imitated the solid-gold hilts. That style became fashionable after the sack of Rome and lasted until about 800, despite the relative fragility of the hilts. With the dawn of the Viking Age came far stronger iron hilts and better blades. Scandinavian fighters most often used double-edged blades intended to be used single-handed.

Damascened swords with iron and steel embellishments have been found buried with the Viking warriors who wielded them.

+ ULFBERHT: MASTER SWORDSMITH +

The best swords of the era bear a trademark of sorts: ULFBERH+T or ULFBERHT+ or other variants. The swords were produced over three hundred years, so the name must refer to a family or a workshop rather than one expert individual. Modern research has discovered that some of the Ulfberht swords used steel with exceptionally high carbon content. The technology for smelting this high-quality steel did not yet exist in Europe, so experts believe it must have been imported from India, Persia, or Central Asia. This type of steel, handled correctly, would result in a sword far harder and tougher than the average European weapon.

Some of the swords bearing the trademark are made of inferior steel, however—pirated copies. One archaeometallurgist discovered that most of the swords marked ULFBERH+T contain the highest quality steel. Accept nothing less.

Of course, the switch to iron doesn't mean the Vikings gave up on aesthetically pleasing swords. Many of the most ornate swords and spheres uncovered in Viking graves are damascened:

decorated with iron and steel wire hammered into elaborate patterns. Master smiths used this technique on spears as well as swords. The Franks excelled in this technique—the Vikings likely learned it from them.

Offense and Defense

Vikings often started their battles with flying arrows and spears, taking out as many of their opponents as possible before getting down to hand-to-hand fighting with axes and swords. The Anglo-Saxon poem "The Battle of Maldon" describes the hail of deadly projectiles: "They let the spears, hard as files, fly from their hands, well-made javelins. Bows were busy. Point pierced shield. The rush of battle was fierce . . ." Vikings also used thicker spears, more like lances, for hand fighting.

For protection, Vikings carried round wooden shields with an iron plate in the center to guard the hand. They formed a wall with their shields to hold the line against attacks, a technique that the Anglo-Saxons adopted, as also described in "The Battle of Maldon." Helmets were relatively rare, simply constructed of metal plates in a conical shape—without horns (see Horned Helmets on page 115 for more information). Chain mail is a rare find in early Viking graves, but toward the end of the Viking Age, mail shirts became more common, as seen in burial grounds and contemporary writings.

Send in the Cavalry

Horses also became more important to warriors in the late
Viking Age, allowing them to mirror on land the speed and
mobility of their ships at sea. Graves dating to the 900s begin
to include horses as well as weaponry. Particularly in Denmark,
tenth-century graves include ornate riding equipment, such as
spurs and stirrups inlaid with silver and copper. The bridle bits

The "wall of shields" Viking defensive technique was later used by Anglo-Saxons in battle.

discovered in Danish graves during this time all follow the T or H shape used by the Magyars in Hungary.

The Magyars were to Eastern Europe what the Vikings were to Western Europe: they swept out of the steppes of Asia and ravaged the countryside and cities, making the most of their superior mobility—thanks to horses, in their case, rather than ships. By the early 900s, the disciplined Magyar mounted troops had reached as far west as Bremen, Germany. This invasion spurred the German king (so to speak) to develop his own cavalry forces, which stopped the Hungarians in 933. This cavalry may have helped the Germans conquer the southern Danish trading town of Hedeby the very next year.

HOW RUSSIA GOT ITS NAME

A hundred years before the start of the Viking Age, Swedes had already begun exploring the lands east of the Baltic Sea. By the mid-700s, many Swedes had permanently settled along rivers in what is now Latvia, Estonia, and western Russia. The local Slavs called the settlers the Rus, which is probably derived from the Finnish word for Swedes, *Ruotsi* —and that name probably came from the Scandinavian *roðr*, meaning a crew of oarsmen. So believe it or not, Russia is named after the Swedes.

The Russian Primary Chronicle, written in the early 1100s, retells the story of how the Vikings came to rule over a large swath of western Russia in about 860, known as "The Legend of the Calling of the Princes." The Vikings (also known as *Varangians* in the local language) had conquered several tribes, who rebelled against them:

> *The tributaries of the Varangians drove them back*
> *beyond the sea and, refusing them further tribute,*

> *set out to govern themselves. There was no law*
> *among them, but tribe rose against tribe. Discord*
> *thus ensued among them, and they began to war one*
> *against another. They said to themselves, "Let us seek*
> *a prince who may rule over us and judge us according*
> *to the Law." They accordingly went overseas to the*
> *Varangian Russes . . . [and] said to the people of Rus,*
> *"Our land is great and rich, but there is no order in it.*
> *Come to rule and reign over us."*

According to the legend, the tribes chose three brothers as rulers: Riurik, Sineus, and Truvor. Riurik's kinsman Oleg (also known as Helgi) succeeded him, followed by Riurik's son Igor (Ingvar). The histories of Oleg and Igor are well documented, and Igor's son Sviatoslav was the first ruler of Russia to have a Slavic name.

The Rus formed a warrior and merchant elite, dominating towns they founded, like Novgorod, and cities they conquered, like Kiev, which became the Rus capital. They spearheaded Viking river trading routes south and east to the Black Sea, the Caspian Sea, and beyond. The Rus assimilated into local Slavic culture within a couple of centuries, and no traces of their original culture remained, not even Scandinavian place-names.

TRADERS AND MERCHANTS

The Vikings had no objection to earning money fairly through trade, but their definition of *fair* got a little complicated. Conquering other tribes and forcing them to pay tribute was part of the game, as were raids along Eastern European rivers and lakes. Fur made up a major part of Scandinavian trade, driving exploration and the establishment of new shipping routes.

The Norwegian chieftain Ottar told his story at King Alfred's court in England in the late 800s, recounting how he sailed from his home at Hålogaland in northern Norway around Nordkapp, the northernmost cape of Norway, to the White Sea in Russia to collect furs, walrus ivory, and reindeer antlers. He had persuaded (presumably by force) the Sami nomads in his home region to pay him a tribute every year that included furs. Ottar then sailed south with his haul to Oslo fjord and to the large trading center of Hedeby in southern Denmark.

The search for furs led the Scandinavians, mainly Swedes, east into Russia, and the desire to dominate the sale of furs and major trade routes took them south all the way to Constantinople and the Byzantine Empire, and even as far as Baghdad.

+ THE VARANGIAN GUARD +

The Vikings attacked Constantinople by way of the Black Sea several times in the late 800s and early 900s, and they must have impressed the Byzantines. (This despite someone leaving runic graffiti inside the cathedral of the Hagia Sophia.) A treaty in 911 between Oleg, the Scandinavian leader of the Rus, and the Byzantine Empire includes a clause allowing Rus soldiers to serve in the empire's army. The Byzantines called all Scandinavians Varangians, and by the late 900s, there was a separate group of them within the imperial guard. By the 1000s, Varangians dominated the imperial guard.

Joining the guard, the emperor's elite bodyguard, became a path to fame and fortune for Scandinavians: many sagas tell stories of Vikings who built their reputations in the East before returning home. The most famous member of the Varangian guard was Harald Sigurdsson, known as the Hard Ruler, who went on to be king of all Norway from 1047–1066. In fact, his attack on England in 1066, while unsuccessful, ended up weakening King Harold of England just as a second invader swept in from the south: Duke William of Normandy, who conquered England

at the Battle of Hastings and whose descendants still sit on the British throne. So really, Kate Middleton has the Vikings to thank for her fabulous royal wedding.

Arab Silver

When Arab merchants began coming north along the Volga River in the late 700s, they brought with them a flood of high-quality silver coins that enticed the Vikings to explore farther south and trace the silver to its source. Sailing down the Volga River to the Caspian Sea, they had to pay tribute to the Bulgars and the Khazars, but it was worth it to have a straight shot to the silver-rich Eastern caliphate, also known as the Abbasid caliphate, and the overland camel-train route to Baghdad. The Vikings brought furs, honey, wax, weapons, and slaves to trade for Arab silver. The enormous volume of trade dropped off in the late 900s, most likely because the silver mines of the caliphate began to run low, even as new mines opened in central Germany.

While it lasted, the Arab trade routes brought floods of silver to Scandinavia: more than sixty thousand Arab coins have been found in Scandinavia, minted in Samarkand, Tashkent, and Baghdad. That doesn't begin to capture the size of the flood, though: since Vikings did not use coins, they

Trade routes brought Arab coins to Scandinavia,
some of which were melted down and recast.

melted down much of their treasure to cast into jewelry (see Jewelry, page 61), which had the advantages of being portable as well as glamorous.

The Slave Trade

Vikings found captives nearly as valuable as gold and silver and other booty. Captured people could be ransomed by their friends and families or, more likely, sold as slaves in a wide range of European markets like the Danish town of Hedeby, Marseille, and Venice. Some stayed to labor in Western Europe or returned with the raiders to the Viking homelands (see Rank and File, page 84 for more on thralls).

Many more were shipped to the Byzantine Empire and the Arab caliphate. Both Byzantium and the caliphate had become dependent on slave labor during their earlier periods of military success, when prisoners of war came easy. The center for the European slave trade was central and Eastern Europe, according to local sources as well as Arab chroniclers, including Ahmad Ibn Fadlan. Vikings managed much of that trade.

EXPLORERS AND SETTLERS

Lands of Opportunity

Vikings didn't leave Scandinavia in search of plunder alone. Many were looking for better farming and trading overseas. For both raiding and settling, their first stop was the British Isles. Scandinavian expeditions to England brought the largest rewards from raiding and also resulted in the largest settlements. England was the one foreign country where Scandinavians took the title of king, ruling minor kingdoms in the 800s such as the Kingdom of York and the Five Boroughs (Derby, Leicester, Lincoln, Nottingham, and Stamford—not Staten Island) and eventually ruling all of England in the early 1000s. Vikings also settled in Ireland after raids, eventually dominating trade in some areas, most notably Dublin. But the stepping stones that eventually led the Vikings across the Atlantic to Iceland, Greenland, and North America lay to the north.

The Scottish Islands

The sparsely populated islands of northern Scotland may look barren to modern eyes, but to the Vikings who eventually settled there, most of them from western Norway, they looked familiar and inviting. The Shetland Islands and the Orkney Islands had plenty of grazing land, rich sea life, and sheltered harbors. And of course, the islands offered a good base for raids to the south. The Orkneys were an especially convenient location for raiders, and the settlements there gave rise to a long line of powerful earls. As mentioned on page 103 (Raiders and Warriors), the *Orkneyinga Saga* tells of Vikings leading raids from the islands until the late 1100s, the tail end of the Viking Age.

Place-names and archaeological finds offer evidence that the Vikings assumed total control of both island groups, taking over from the indigenous Picts. Norway maintained political control of the Orkneys until 1468 and the Shetlands until 1469, when they were added to the dowry of the Danish princess Margrethe upon her marriage to King James III of Scotland. The Scandinavian-influenced dialect, Norn, survived well past that point, into the 1700s. The last known speaker died in 1850.

MODERN VIKINGS

The Shetland Islands town of Lerwick celebrates its Viking history every January with a massive fire festival called Up Helly Aa. In its current form, the festival started in the mid-1800s, but its roots date back to the Viking holiday of Yule, which celebrated the return of the sun. It begins in the morning with a parade through town and continues with a torchlight procession of Lerwegians wearing Viking garb, known as guizers (from *disguise*). The head of the festival, the guizer jarl, leads the procession. The highlight of the festival is the chance to throw lit torches at a full-size replica Viking ship and burn it to the ground. The party goes all night—the next day is thankfully an official holiday.

Land of the Faeroes

The steep-sided, treeless Faeroe Islands are the tops of an underwater mountain range that connects Scotland and Iceland, but on top of the shore cliffs, settlers found green fields and mild weather thanks to the Gulf Stream, ideal grazing conditions for sheep. Viking settlers may have stumbled upon the islands

studied the sun, moon, and stars, as well as the flight paths of birds, Flóki went one step further and brought three ravens on board his ship, asking the gods to bless them. When he had sailed well out to sea, he released the ravens. One flew toward the Faeroe Islands, one flew straight up and returned to the ship, and one flew forward, leading him to the coast of Iceland. After that, he became known as Hrafna-Flóki, or Raven Flóki.

Once he reached Iceland, Flóki acted a bit less strategically. He and his crew were distracted by the excellent fishing in Breidafjord and forgot to harvest hay—that winter, all their livestock starved to death. The spring was cold: the sea ice lingered, and bad weather forced him to spend the next winter on Borgarfjord. The disillusioned explorer decided to name the land Iceland. The name stuck, but other travelers gave better reports, and by 870 hopeful settlers began arriving on Iceland's shores.

Viking Pioneers

With earthquakes, hot springs, geysers, and active volcanoes, Iceland must have seemed like an alien planet. But the fjords and glaciers echoed the Norwegian landscape, and there were good grazing lands, forests of dwarf birch and willow trees, and plenty of driftwood for carpentry.

The first Scandinavians who traveled to Iceland intending to settle there were two brothers, Ingolf and Hjorleif. They scouted the east fjords in the late 860s and returned in 870 to settle permanently. Ari Thorgilsson recorded their story circa 1120–1130 in *Íslendingabók, The Book of the Icelanders*. Hjorleif's Irish slaves killed him during the first winter, but Ingolf spent three years exploring and finally established himself at Reykjavík.

More settlers soon followed. Most came from western and northern Norway, but others came from Viking outposts in Scotland and Ireland, along with their Celtic wives and Celtic slaves. According to *Íslendingabók* and archaeological finds, the coasts and southern plains were completely settled by 930. The Icelanders built turf houses, since there were no large trees for construction, and made their living farming, fishing, and trading on risky but frequent voyages to the Faeroes, Norway, and the British Isles.

Live Free or Die

Landnámabók, The Book of Settlements, lists about 430 leaders of individual settlements, their ancestors, and their descendants. It was written in the 1100s, at the end of the Viking Age, and while it presents itself as a history book, its likely goal was to establish the legitimacy of the families currently in power. The named settlers were mostly local chieftains from Norway who brought their families and followers with them.

MODERN VIKINGS

Early settlers brought horses from Norway to Iceland, and in 982 the Althing government banned the importation of horses. This law has always been enforced, and it is still in effect to protect the breed from diseases. Once an Icelandic horse leaves the country, it may never return. For more than a thousand years, the Icelandic breed has evolved in isolation, making it one of the purest horse breeds on earth. The horses aren't snobby about their impeccable pedigrees, though: they're shaggy, sturdy little horses with lively, friendly personalities.

Where most horses have three main gaits—walk, trot, and canter or gallop—the Icelandic has five. The fourth is the *tölt*, a four-beat ambling gait in which only one foot at a time touches the ground—very useful on rough terrain. The fifth is the *skeið*, or flying pace, similar to a smooth, fast trot with a moment of suspension between footfalls. This pace takes some training to learn and is highly prized, while the *tölt* comes naturally.

At the time the book was written, the authors believed that the settlers struck out for Iceland to escape the tyranny of King Harald Finehair, who unified much of Norway. But since he died in 930 and was reportedly only sixteen winters old when Ingolf first explored Iceland, he couldn't have been the only motivation, or even the main one. Still it's telling that Iceland, like the Faeroes and Greenland, never had a king or an earl and that all three regions remained republics of leading farmers until well after the Viking Age.

In the early years, disputes often escalated into drawn-out blood feuds. Driven to find a more organized system of justice, they turned to the old Scandinavian custom of meetings known as *things*, where any free man could defend his rights. In 930, the first Althing took place, a national assembly or parliament. They chose an inland location, now called Thingvellir, that had many practical points to recommend it: it was accessible by land from all corners of Iceland and located on a wide plain where hundreds of people could gather and camp. And somehow the Icelanders were also drawn to select the rift valley where the North American and Eurasian tectonic plates are slowly pulling apart. Talk about an epic vibe. Today, Thingvellir is Iceland's only UNESCO World Heritage site.

The Althing seems to have been organized by an interlinked family dynasty, making it more of an oligarchy than a republic. Thirty-six chieftains formed the voting body of the

Althing, dividing the power among themselves. Over time, the Icelanders developed a lengthy catalog of laws, later (oddly) known as *Grágás*, or Gray Goose. The laws were not actually written down until 1118, so for the first couple hundred years, the laws remained a purely oral tradition. The lawspeaker, who presided over the legislature, had to memorize all the laws before taking office. During his three-year term, he would recite one-third of the laws every year at the Althing.

MODERN VIKINGS

The Isle of Man is strategically located in the middle of the Irish Sea; the Vikings conquered and settled there in the mid-800s, early in the Viking Age. Their legacy lives on in the island's unique role in the United Kingdom: it remains technically independent, with the British monarch holding the additional title Lord of Man, and it has its own parliament called the Tynwald. This name comes from the Old Norse *Þingvollr*, the same root as Iceland's Thingvellir. No one knows for sure how long the Tynwald has been meeting, but every year, the members gather on a man-made hill, Tynwald Hill, along with representatives of the British monarch and the Church of England, to ratify the laws passed over the past year.

To settle their differences, Vikings held things,
or assemblies. The largest was the Althing, which
took place in Thingvellir in Iceland.

The Althing has continued to meet almost without inter-ruption to this day, even through the Icelandic civil war in the 1200s. The only break lasted from 1799 to 1844 under Danish colonial rule. This record makes the Althing the oldest and longest-running parliament in the world.

Concentration of Power

Perhaps the high point of Iceland's parliamentary system was the peaceful establishment of Christianity as the country's official religion in the year 1000. Christianization in other Scandinavian and European countries was often characterized by rampant violence and civil war. The Christian and pagan fac-tions in Iceland agreed to a compromise in which all Icelanders would be baptized, but pagans could practice their religious rituals in private. These rights were later withdrawn, but the compromise saw the country through the transition.

The low point came in the mid-1200s when the concen-tration of power in the hands of a few wealthy families led to unrest, and eventually to civil war. The mounting instability and violence inspired Iceland's greatest writers and poets to look back toward the "good old days" of the early settlements. The great sagas were written during this time. The family sagas in particular, loosely based on the first settlers, have a strikingly modern style and realistic characters. *Njal's Saga*, *Egil's Saga*, and a few others have earned a place among the great works of European literature. In 1263, Icelanders turned to the king of Norway to restore order and gave up their cherished independence. The literary tradition began to decline soon after.

+ THE OLD GODS AND THE NEW +

When Iceland officially adopted Christianity by a vote of the Althing in the year 1000, the lawspeaker happened to be a pagan named Thorgeir. To demonstrate his commitment to the decision, Thorgeir went home to northern Iceland and cast his pagan idols into a huge waterfall, ever after known as Goðafoss, the waterfall of the gods.

Although the Icelandic sagas were written after the rise of Christianity, they are the most important source of information about Viking gods and religious practices. No other Germanic people kept such records of their pagan past, but Iceland's fascination with family history and the settlement period allowed Christian descendants to remember their pagan ancestors with pride.

ACROSS THE
NORTH ATLANTIC

The dangers of the North Atlantic were the stuff of legend, but the Viking sense of adventure pushed them past fear. The historian and cleric Adam of Bremen wrote in 1076 about the ill-fated voyage of exploration that some Frisian sailors took north of Iceland:

> *Of a sudden they fell into that numbing ocean's dark mist which could hardly be penetrated with the eyes. And, behold, the current of the fluctuating ocean whirled back to its mysterious fountainhead and with most furious impetuosity drew the unhappy sailors, who in their despair now thought only of death, on to chaos; this they say is the abysmal chasm—that deep in which, report has it, all the back flow of the sea, which appears to decrease, is absorbed and in turn revomited, as the mounting fluctuation is usually described. As the partners were imploring the mercy of God to receive their souls, the backward thrust of the sea carried away some of their ships, but its forward ejection threw the rest far behind the others. Freed thus by the timely help of God from the instant*

> *peril they had before their eyes, they seconded the*
> *flood by rowing with all their might.*

Heading into the unknown on scarcely more than rumor and instinct may have been a dangerous business, but the Vikings had enough confidence in their own resourcefulness to try it over and over again.

Some of the Vikings' greatest accomplishments started by getting hopelessly lost. Many of the sagas use the evocative expression *hafvilla* to describe a state of completely losing one's sense of direction. In *Finnboga Saga*, we read the ominous phrase *"tekr af byri, ok gerir á fyrir beim hafvillur"* ("the fair wind failed, and they wholly lost their reckoning"). Emerging from storm or fog, many lost sailors sighted lands that inspired them or those who came after to explore new lands and boldly go where no one had gone before.

Greenland: The Real Ice Land

The first person to lay eyes on Greenland was a sailor blown far off course on a voyage from Norway to Iceland around the year 900. His name was Gunnbjörn Ulf-Krakuson. And while that amazing name sounds like it means "bear with a gun, son of the wolf and the kraken," it actually means something more like "battle bear, son of wolf-Slender Man"—equally terrifying.

In any case, he gave the name Gunnbjörn's Skerries to the bare rocks he sighted.

Many years later, Eirik the Red, so named for his hair, beard, and hot temper, took a circuitous route back to those barren rocks. As an adolescent around 980, he and his father had to flee their home in Jaeren, southwest Norway, after "some killings." They immigrated to Iceland—but more killings got

What seemed like a heap of barren rocks, Gunnbjörn's Skerries was actually the first glimpse of Greenland.

him banished a few years later. Eirik took to the sea again with several followers, this time in search of Gunnbjörn's Skerries. He may not have been flying blind: from where he lived in northwest Iceland, the mountains of Greenland become visible in summer through a mirage effect.

Eirik spotted land near the skerries on the east coast and continued south along the forbidding, icy shore and around

Cape Farewell. On the west coast, he discovered sheltered fjords and good pastureland. After three years of exploring, he sailed back to Iceland to drum up a group of settlers. He called the land Greenland, saying, "Men would be much more eager to go there if the land had an attractive name." It helped that land was already becoming scarce in Iceland.

Around 985, Eirik sailed for Greenland with a group of twenty-five ships. Some turned back, some disappeared along the way, and eventually fourteen made it to the new land. Eirik claimed a farm along Eiriksfjord, which he called Brattahlið— some of the most fertile land in Greenland. The Eiriksfjord area became known as the Eastern Settlement, with the Western Settlement established soon after, three hundred miles farther northwest. Eirik had set himself up well: from twice-outlawed, potentially sociopathic fugitive to chieftain in his own land.

Living on the Edge

The Eastern and Western Settlements peaked in the 1350s at around 280 farms and 16 Christian churches. Population estimates vary from fifteen hundred people up to six thousand, but in any case, such a small outpost was always vulnerable to epidemics and violence. One of the bodies buried at the first church in Brattahlið actually still had a dagger stuck between his ribs when archaeologists dug him up.

In the ocean there are very many islands, of which not the least is Greenland, situated far out in the ocean opposite the mountains of Sweden . . . To this island, they say, it is from five to seven days' sail from the coast of Norway, the same as to Iceland. The people there are greenish from the salt water, whence, too, that region gets its name. The people live in the same manner as the Icelanders, except that they are fiercer and trouble seafarers by their piratical attacks.

—Adam of Bremen, providing an alternate explanation for the name Greenland

In the treeless landscape, Greenlanders built their homes out of turf with driftwood roofs, construction techniques they had learned in Iceland. The farms mostly supported sheep, goats, and cows. One advantage Greenland had over Iceland was better grazing land: farmers had never lived there, while Iceland's soil had deteriorated after a hundred years of heavy use. They traveled farther north, to fish and hunt seals, reindeer, hares, and game birds. Archaeological evidence of their travels has been found as far north as Ellesmere Island in Canada.

The northern hunting grounds provided trade goods as well, since necessities like timber, iron, tools, and corn had to be imported. The settlers exported furs, walrus ivory, falcons, and even polar bears. Greenlanders also sold narwhal horns for serious money: in medieval Europe, they were believed to be unicorn horns full of powerful magic. The Greenlanders probably didn't believe the myth, having plenty of chances to see live and beached narwhals, which means they directly contributed

Narwhal tusks fetched a nice price from Europeans, thanks to their resemblance to the mythical unicorn's horn.

to the disillusionment of millions of grade-school girls who will discover one day that unicorns aren't real.

The Greenlanders spun their own thread and wove their own cloth, as most Viking farms did. In fact, the best example of a Viking Age loom was discovered in Greenland, in the ruins of a farm that was covered in sand and then buried in permafrost. The Farm Beneath the Sand, as it's now known, had a room dedicated to weaving and spinning that was in use the entire time the farm was occupied, from the early 1000s to about 1400. Analysis of the cloth revealed that it contained fibers from farm animals (sheep, goats, cattle), but also wild animals like caribou, arctic fox, polar bear, brown bear, and bison. Now, brown bears and bison have never lived in Greenland. So this hair could have come from Europe or possibly also from North America. Either the settlers sailed to North America to hunt, or they traded with the Inuit.

The New World

Once again *hafvilla* and blind chance played their roles in a major Viking discovery. *Saga of the Greenlanders* credits Bjarni Herjólfsson with being the first to sight North America. Around 985, as he was attempting to trace Eirik the Red's route, he was blown off course in the fog and spotted a flat, thickly forested land—clearly not Greenland. While he didn't stop to explore, he inspired Leif Eirikson, Leif the

Bjarni Herjólfsson's view in 985 might have looked like this. His accounts of a forested land inspired other Viking explorers to set out at sea. They eventually landed in North America.

Lucky, son of Eirik the Red. Perhaps predictably, *The Saga of Eirik the Red* ignores Bjarni and gives all the credit of discovery to Leif. But the sagas agree that Leif was first to set foot in this new land.

Leif Eirikson sailed first to Helluland, or Flat Stone Land, which was likely southern Baffin Island, then south to Markland, Forest Land, which scholars believe was the east coast of Labrador. Two days southwest, Leif landed in Vinland, possibly Vine Land or Berry Land. He built shelter for the winter here and sailed back to Greenland in the spring to tell his tale. His brother Thorwald set out on his own expedition, fired up by Leif's stories. He encountered the first North Americans the Vikings had seen and was killed by an arrow during a skirmish. Thorfinn Karlsefni also attempted to settle in Vinland, where his wife, Gudrid, gave birth to their son, Snorri, the first European born in North America. However, the would-be settlers gave up after three winters of being harassed by the locals, whom the Vikings dubbed Skraelinger.

The location of the legendary Vinland has long been debated, with its wild grapevines and wheat and snow-free winters. It may have been near the Gulf of Saint Lawrence, which is as far north as wild vines can grow. But the stories of grapes might have been added later based on a medieval interpretation of the name Vinland.

Archaeologists have uncovered one Viking settlement that definitively proves the Scandinavians made it to North America. On the northern tip of Newfoundland, at L'Anse aux Meadows, lie the ruins of large buildings with turf walls, typical Icelandic or Greenlandic construction, and an array of Viking-era artifacts. There isn't any evidence of farming or livestock, and the buildings seem to have been used only for short periods of time.

What L'Anse aux Meadows might have looked like in its heyday.

It seems likely that L'Anse aux Meadows was more of a base camp for expeditions farther south, where Vinland may have been located. In any case, no other Viking farms have been discovered in North America. Such a remote colony, an offshoot of another remote colony, could not have depended on support or regular trade with fellow Scandinavians. It's not surprising that the settlements didn't take root.

A Five-Hundred-Year Experiment

Greenland depended on trade with Iceland, and to some extent Norway, as we've seen. The ties were always weak, given the risky nature of sailing in the North Atlantic. In the 1200s, life began to get still harder. The climate began to shift, growing slowly colder. Greenlanders also saw their cherished independence getting chipped away. After Iceland came under Norwegian rule in the mid-1200s, the settlers in Greenland were forbidden to own ships. They couldn't very well defy the ban, and life became even more precarious as they waited for others to bring the wood and iron they needed. Fewer merchants found it worthwhile to make the trip, though: the demand for walrus ivory slowed as Portugal and other European countries began importing elephant ivory from Africa. And while the Black Death never hit Greenland, it took out half the population of Norway, a major trading partner, in the mid-1300s.

The Western Settlement was deserted by the 1350s, when a priest visited from the Eastern Settlement and found only abandoned farms and near-feral livestock. The Eastern Settlement lingered maybe 150 years longer. The last written record is from 1408, when a couple named Sigrid Bjornsdottir and Thorstein Olafsson got married in the Hvalseye church—and then moved to Iceland. In the early 1600s, when King Christian IV of Denmark and Norway sent expeditions to the island, there were no Scandinavians left in Greenland.

Speculation on the reason for the Vikings' disappearance runs rampant: from Inuit attacks, to a conservative refusal to adopt a new diet, to the idea that some survivors got jobs as fishermen on English ships in North America. But evidence provides several indications that the Vikings packed up and left Greenland in a calm, orderly fashion. There are no mass graves or groupings of unburied bodies, as a plague or attack would suggest. Archaeologists have found the bodies of farm animals, likely abandoned when their owners sailed away, since the animals weren't eaten. And no items of any real value, like swords or silver Communion cups, have turned up in the ruins. It seems the Vikings just realized it was time to move on.

VALHALLA

GODS AND THE
AFTERLIFE

THE WORLD OF THE GODS

Creation Myths

The Vikings understood their universe as a series of interlinked worlds, ruled by gods who acted a lot like hot-tempered, high-handed humans, and threatened by all kinds of monsters and mischievous spirits. There's a lot more to Norse mythology than you might have learned from superhero movies. We'll break down the setup of the worlds here and get into gods and monsters in the next chapters: everyone from the Aesir to the Valkyries.

In the beginning was Ginnungagap, the great void, which was ice in the north and fire in the south. Where the fire and ice met, water droplets formed Ymir the giant. The first man and woman grew from under his arm, and the first frost giants grew from under his feet. His cow licked the ice until she released another being, Buri, the grandfather of Odin.

Odin and his brothers killed Ymir and created the Norse world: they turned his skull into the sky, his blood into the sea, and his flesh and bones into the earth. The earth they created had several realms, all connected by Yggdrasil, the world ash tree:

- **ASGARD**: The home of the gods. It was connected to the human world by Bifröst, the rainbow bridge. Beneath the

In Viking lore, the world ash tree, Yggdrasil, connected the realms of gods, monsters, and men.

root of Yggdrasil in this world lay the sacred spring of fate, the well of Urd.

+ **MIDGARD:** The human realm, sometimes translated as Middle Earth. It was surrounded by a sea where the world serpent, Jörmungandr, encircled the land, biting his own tail.

+ **UTGARD:** The outer realm beyond the sea, home of giants. Beneath the root of Yggdrasil, here was the sacred spring of wisdom, the spring of Mimir. The giants' realm was also known as Jotunheim. (Also the name of a mountain range and national park in Norway, home to the country's highest mountains.)

+ **NIFLHEIM:** The underworld below Midgard, the land of mists, home of people who died in bed or from disease.

ODIN

One-Eyed Snake

As the world's greatest pirates, naturally the Vikings worshipped a one-eyed god. Odin, the head of the Aesir family of gods, was the mystical, unpredictable god of wisdom, poetry, and battle. His pet ravens, Hugin and Munin, flew around the world every day and brought him the news. His favorite weapon was the spear, and he rode an eight-legged horse named Sleipnir. He was also known as the All Father, God of Cargoes, Father of Battle, and God of Hanged Men. This last nickname is tied to the picturesque custom of hanging dead bodies in the trees around Norse temples as sacrifices to Odin. Yes, that includes dead humans.

Apparently Odin was a bit of a masochist: he sacrificed his eye to drink from the spring of wisdom; he hung himself for nine days from Yggdrasil, the tree at the center of the world, in order to learn the secret meaning of runes; and once, he took on the shape of a giant snake to seduce a giant's daughter into giving him the mead of inspiration. Did we mention he was married? We hardly know anything about his wife, Frigg, but she must have been very patient.

Not surprisingly, people hardly ever named their children after Odin.

SOON WE SHALL BE DRINKING ALE FROM CURVED HORNS. THE CHAMPION WHO COMES INTO ODIN'S DWELLING DOES NOT LAMENT HIS DEATH. . . . I LAUGH AS I DIE.

—THE DEATH SONG OF RAGNAR LOÐBRÓK

Valhalla and the Valkyries

As the god of battle, Odin had the Valkyries to carry out his commands in the human realm. These fierce females wore armor and rode on horseback over land and sea, granting victory as Odin saw fit. After the battle, they chose the cream of the crop to escort to Odin's great hall, Valhalla. Life as Odin's guest was the best of all worlds in a Viking's eyes: the warriors battled all day, and then the dead came back to life in time to feast and drink all night.

THOR

Days of Thunder

Mjollnir, Thor's hammer

Odin's son Thor was the Viking-est of all the Viking deities, and the most popular. The myths show him as a hot-tempered, straightforward, enormously strong god with a fiery red beard. He ruled over thunder and lightning, wind and rain, and people called upon him to grant fair weather for sea voyages and farming. His most famous accessory is of course his hammer, Mjollnir, but to get fully decked out, he had his iron gloves, a girdle of strength, and a cart pulled by goats.

Fish Tale

As the defender of Asgard, Thor had many enemies: he often fought giants and had a long-running feud with Jörmungandr, the world serpent or Midgard serpent, who lay under the sea, coiled around the world, biting its own tail. One of the best-loved and most retold Viking myths is the story of Thor's fishing trip with the giant Hymir. When Thor asked where to find bait, Hymir sent him out to the pasture to dig worms, but instead Thor saw the giant's big black ox and ripped its head off to bait his hook.

Thor rowed far out to sea, where Hymir caught two whales right away. Thor's competitive side came out: he tossed out his ox-head bait and hooked none other than the Midgard serpent. The sea monster pulled so hard that Thor's feet pushed through the boat, and he had to brace himself against the bottom of the sea.

Then, as the old story goes in "Hymir's Poem," "the sea-wolf shrieked and the underwater rocks re-echoed, all the ancient earth was collapsing." Thor paid no attention to the apocalypse he was triggering and raised his hammer to strike the final blow—but Hymir panicked and cut the line. Thor tossed him overboard for ruining the greatest fish story ever told.

Hammer of the Gods

Thor's hammer was everywhere in the Viking world: on rune stones, in poetry, and in carvings. Hammer-shaped pendants were the most common jewelry for men. In his sacred temples, people took oaths on arm rings dedicated to him. And we know, from a rather Bugs Bunnyish myth, that Mjollnir also made an appearance in wedding ceremonies.

One day, Thor couldn't find his hammer, and he enlisted Loki to look for it. Loki went out searching in falcon form and discovered that the giant Thrym had hidden the hammer deep underground and refused to give it back unless the gods gave him Freyja as his wife. They came up with a plan to get the hammer back and save Freyja: Thor would hide his beard and biceps under a bridal veil and go to the wedding disguised as the goddess, with Loki dressed up as his maid.

At the feast before the wedding, the giants were a little startled to watch the bride inhale an ox and eight whole salmon, but Loki explained she was so excited for the wedding that she hadn't eaten in eight days. Thrym tried to kiss the bride, but was scared off by her burning eyes glaring through the veil. Again Loki explained that she was so excited for the wedding that she hadn't slept in eight days.

Thor undercover as Freyja,
hoping to fool the giant Thrym.

When Thor's hammer was brought in for the traditional blessing and laid in the bride's lap, the wedding turned into something out of *Game of Thrones*. Thor grabbed the hammer, killed the entire wedding party with it, tore off the bloody bridal veil, and walked out.

MODERN VIKINGS

Scandinavian parents today have about five hundred variations of the name Thor to choose from for their baby boys and girls. (To compare, we found about fourteen Odin-related names.) For literary types, there's Tove, as in Tove Jansson, the Finnish author of the beloved Moomins series. For aspiring stage moms, there's Thora, as in former child actress Thora Birch. For the bloodthirsty, there's Tormund, after the fiery red-bearded Wildling from *Game of Thrones*. And for moms and dads with a sadistic sense of humor, we give you Thorlacius.

FREY AND FREYJA

Thor's popularity meant he was invoked at important moments like weddings and planting time, but pagans had plenty of options. The main Scandinavian fertility gods were the brother and sister Frey and Freyja. They belonged to the earthy family of gods known as the Vanir, while Odin and Thor belonged to the Aesir.

Frey

Frey's domain overlapped with his sister's: farming and fertility. People made offerings to him at weddings, and he had the power to grant peace and prosperity. Ritual feasts and performances were held in his honor, which sometimes included human sacrifice.

Frey had some cool sidekicks, like the golden boar Gullinbursti, and the ship *Skiðblaðnir*, which was large enough to hold all the gods but could be folded up and kept in a pouch— who doesn't love friends with boats? But by far the most appropriate companion for a fertility god was a huge, majestic stallion. Frey's horse, Freyfaxi, appears in many Icelandic sagas and is associated with tales of horse competitions and horse fighting. Several statues of Frey discovered around Scandinavia indicate that the fertility god might have shared certain . . . physical attributes with the horse.

Freyja

Freyja driving her chariot pulled by cats. Seriously!

Freyja was the goddess of love, beauty, fertility, and magic. She drove a chariot pulled by two cats, could take the shape of a bird, and wore the legendary necklace Brisingamen. Beautiful witchy cat lady with Liz Taylor–worthy jewels? Sign us up for that cult.

Many of the myths about Freyja involve a threat of kidnapping her or handing her over as someone's (usually a giant's) bride, and the gods have to come up with a plan to get her out of it. This shows that women of the Viking Age had every reason to suspect they could be treated like booty (in both the pirate sense and the hip-hop sense). But the stories also contain the idea, refreshing for the Dark Ages, that women had every right to be furious about it.

OTHER GODS AND GODDESSES

LOKI: A trickster and troublemaker. He sometimes came to the aid of the other gods, but usually to untangle a problem he caused in the first place. He's a comic scene stealer in myths and folktales about Odin and Thor and many other gods, but there's no evidence of people actually worshipping him. He could take on many forms, including a bird, a fly, a salmon, an old woman, and more. Once, while disguised as a mare, he actually got pregnant and gave birth to Odin's famous steed, the eight-legged Sleipnir. He had a dark side, though: with the giantess Angrboða, he fathered Hel, goddess of the underworld; the giant wolf Fenrir; and the world serpent, Thor's old enemy, Jörmungandr.

SIF: Thor's wife, associated with the harvest. Loki cut off her fair hair in a fit of mischief and had to go on a quest to replace it with hair of actual gold.

FRIGG: Odin's wife and the mother of Thor and Baldur. She was invoked by Viking women for protection during childbirth.

BALDUR: A son of Odin and Frigg, renowned for his beauty and goodness. His death led directly to Ragnarök, the destruction of the world.

IDUN: A goddess who guarded the apples that kept the Aesir forever young. She and her apples might have been borrowed from Irish mythology.

NJORD: A fertility god of the sea and sailors, a member of the Vanir family of gods, and father of Frey and Freyja. He lived in the hall called Noátun ("enclosure of ships"), and he was mainly worshipped along the west coast of Norway.

SKADI: A huntress from the mountains who chose a husband from the gods as recompense when the gods killed her father, a giant. The gods hid so she could only see their feet—she thought she was choosing the handsome Baldur, but she picked Njord. She never felt at home in the sea, so she went back to the mountains and lived on her own, where she could ski and shoot arrows to her heart's content. Like Dolly Parton, she's the queen of starting over again.

TYR: An ancient god of war with only one hand. Tyr lost the hand while magically binding the monster wolf Fenrir. As Loki's son, the wolf was raised in Asgard, but he grew up to be so fierce that only Tyr was brave enough to feed him. The gods knew he had to be tied up, but he was too strong for any chain to hold. At last Odin taught the dwarves to craft an unbreakable chain, forged from the secret things of the world: the breath of a fish, the noise of a moving cat, and the roots of a mountain. It looked as fine as silk, and the gods convinced Fenrir to let them lay it around his neck—as long as one of them put a hand between his teeth as a hostage. Only Tyr was brave enough to volunteer. When Fenrir couldn't break the chain, Tyr paid the price.

HEL: Goddess of the underworld, and Loki's daughter. Her dark, misty kingdom, Niflheim, surrounded by a high wall, was where men went when they died of disease or old age. Not much to look forward to—that might help to explain a Viking's willingness to die on the battlefield.

HEIMDALL: The watcher who guarded Bifröst, the rainbow bridge to Asgard, against the frost giants. He could see farther than an eagle, and his ears were sharp enough to hear grass growing on earth. His horn, Gjallarhorn, was loud enough to be heard through all the worlds. He was the son of nine maidens, however that works.

+ THE DAYS OF THE WEEK +

DAY	ORIGIN
Sunday	sun's day
Monday	moon's day
Tuesday	Tyr's day
Wednesday	Odin's day
Thursday	Thor's day
Friday	Frey or Freyja's day
Saturday	wash day

THE NORNS: The three goddesses of fate, named Urðr (fate), Verðandi (being), and Skuld (necessity). They stood separate from the Aesir and Vanir families of the gods; mortals, Valkyries, and gods alike had to submit to their decisions. Scandinavians knew better than to try to change fate by sucking up to the Norns—there's no evidence of sacrifices made to them.

EVERYTHING BUT THE HOBBITS

In addition to unreliable, sometimes selfish gods, the Viking world was full of mischievous or downright malignant spirits—any farm or road could have a special rock or mound nearby that couldn't be disturbed because something supernatural lived there. All these entities had to be constantly appeased with gifts, sacrifices, chants, etc. The whole thing sounds exhausting.

GIANTS: The frenemies of the gods, giants sometimes fought the gods, kidnapped them, and stole their treasures. But just as often gods and giants married and had children together. There were mountain giants, frost giants, fire giants, and probably more. They lived in Utgard, the outer lands.

ELVES: They lived in the kingdom of Alfheim and could also be found living in mounds in the earth. Scandinavians sacrificed animals and offered the meat to the elves—sounds a little more bloodthirsty than *The Lord of the Rings*.

MODERN VIKINGS

The elves haven't been forgotten in Iceland. Studies in 1998 and 2007 revealed that more than half of Icelanders believe it's possible that the elves of the folktales are still living among them. A former member of Parliament swears that elves saved his life in a crash on a remote road. Often, road construction has been halted or moved to preserve "elf rocks." Press inquiries about this are so common that the Icelandic Road and Coastal Administration has a five-page official missive it sends out in response. A professor of folklore at the University of Iceland collected stories of what happens when elves are disturbed during construction: machines break, workers have accidents or get sick. They sound a little like American gremlins— no word yet on what happens when you feed an elf after midnight.

DWARVES: Clever and cunning, the dwarves lived in isolated places away from humans. They were excellent craftsmen and made many of the gods' treasures.

DÍSIR: These mysterious beings represented fertility in people and in nature, led by Freyja, the goddess of love. They were worshipped mostly in Sweden.

TROLLS: Any visitor to Scandinavia is surrounded by adorably ugly trolls, from tiny figurines in souvenir shops to children's books to garden statues. But although the word *troll* or *trold* appears in the *Prose Edda*, it could describe giants, elves, or generally hostile spirits—and the *Prose Edda* was written a hundred years or more after the end of the Viking Age.

The folklore around trolls developed during the Middle Ages, contrasting the ugly, vicious trolls with good Christians. Troll stories really took off in the 1800s, when regional folklore was all the rage across Europe. Asbjørnsen and Moe, the brothers Grimm of Norway, published a popular collection of fairy tales in 1879 that often featured troll villains.

PAGAN RITUALS

Temple Worship

What we know about Viking religious rituals comes from an incomplete patchwork of contemporary Viking writings, accounts written by outsiders, and archaeology. In general, Viking religion was decentralized and varied from region to region, with many worship practices taking place in private homes or outdoors.

Uppsala today is a major cultural center in Sweden, home to Scandinavia's largest cathedral and oldest university. In the Viking Age, it hosted large religious feasts for Thor, Odin, and Frey in an elaborate temple, though the only relics now are large mounds. Lejre, near Roskilde in Denmark, had another temple site, this one marked by stones laid out in the shape of a ship, more than eighty yards long, and a very large hall. These feasts were likely under royal control; there doesn't seem to have been a dedicated priest class in the Viking religion.

Separate accounts written in the mid-1000s by German Christians about each location give remarkably similar descriptions of the rituals. In both temples, people gathered every nine years for human and animal sacrifices. At Lejre, the sacrifices were ninety-nine people and ninety-nine horses, dogs, and chickens; at Uppsala, it was nine of every kind of male creature, and the corpses were hung in the trees near the temple.

There isn't much physical evidence of the rituals associated with sacrifices or honoring the gods, but the tapestry found in the Oseberg ship burial in Norway depicts what might be a religious procession. It shows people on horseback, in wagons, and on foot, some carrying weapons and one wearing an animal mask. Carvings of animal masks have been found in Sweden, and two

actual masks were found in the excavation of Hedeby's harbor in
Denmark: a small dog or possibly a sheep, and a large ox head.

+ WITCHY WOMEN +

The narrator of the poem *Völuspá*, who tells the
story of Ragnarök, is the most famous example
of a *völva* practicing her magic arts. The *völva*'s
form of divination, known as *seiðr*, was inspired
and spread by the goddess Freyja. Led by the
female seeress, seated high on a platform, the
seiðr ritual involved a choir singing spells and
sending the *völva* into an ecstatic trance. With
the power of the spells channeling through her,
she could answer questions about the future like
a Greek oracle.

Try This at Home

Gods and spirits could be worshipped outside, in groves, at
springs, or on top of mountains. In Sweden and Denmark, ship
settings like the stone outline in Lejre may have been places of
worship, judging from excavated firepits. Archaeologists have
found sacrifices of bent swords and other deliberately broken

In addition to animals, Viking gods would accept swords bent and wound in sacrifice.

weapons thrown into marshes in southeastern Sweden, in Uppland and on the island of Gotland.

The Spanish Arab al-Tartushi visited the Danish market town of Hedeby in the late 900s and told of a feast in honor of "the god." Any family who sacrificed an animal hung up the carcass outside their house to show their devotion. No word on whether the public displays of bigger and better animals ever led to chicken shaming.

Elves got their share of attention as well. The Norwegian Christian poet Sigvat Thordarson came across an elf sacrifice in a private home in the 1020s while searching for a place to stay the night in Sweden—but he wasn't invited in.

> *"No farther can you enter,*
> *You wretch!" said the woman.*
> *"Here we are heathens*
> *And I fear the wrath of Odin."*
> *She shoved me out like a wolf,*
> *That arrogant termagant,*
> *Said she was holding sacrifice*
> *To elves there in her house.*

Ship Funerals

Hollywood's idea of a Viking funeral is a dead king laid to rest in a longship and pushed out to sea, with flaming arrows sent after him until the whole ship catches fire in a great floating funeral pyre that sails over the horizon. It's a majestic image, but it's based on a mixed-up understanding of Viking funerals, and there's no written or archaeological record of it ever happening. The Old English poem *Beowulf* shows one example of a burial ship sent off to sea, but it was not set on fire, and the poem wasn't written by Vikings, so never mind.

The Vikings saw death as another journey and equipped their dead accordingly. Hundreds of people buried in ships have been found all over Scandinavia, from small rowboats to the richly ornamented Oseberg ship. Sometimes the ship was burned in a huge funeral pyre, and sometimes it was covered with a huge mound that served as a memorial. The graves often included weapons, tools, jewelry, and other fine possessions, as well as food and drink. Even the poor might be buried with a prized knife and surrounded by a ship setting: stones laid out in a symbolic outline of a ship.

Signs of the Cross

Christianity spread slowly through Scandinavia through-out the Viking Age, and some customs mingled in funeral

MODERN VIKINGS

The pagan spirit is alive and well in Iceland. The ancient religion of the Vikings, the first Icelandic settlers, was officially recognized by the government in 1973 with the official name Ásatrú. It's now Iceland's fastest-growing religion, with more than thirty-five hundred members, and recently topped 1 percent of the population (yes, it's a small country). The central organization, Ásatrúarfélagið, performs weddings, funerals, and name-giving ceremonies for children, in addition to celebrating six feast days known as *blót*, honoring the Norse gods as well as natural events such as the winter solstice. They have formally rejected any connection with extremist right-wing "pagans" internationally, whose beliefs are shaped by the same misinterpretations of the Norse gods that inspired the Nazis. Ásatrúarfélagið is currently building the first pagan temple in a thousand years, on a hillside above Reykjavík.

rites. Several graves have been uncovered across Scandinavia that mix symbols of the Christian cross with symbols of Thor's hammer, or with grave goods, which were forbidden in Christian burials. One artisan in northern Denmark left behind a mold with spaces to cast a Christian cross and Thor's hammer side by side. The Vikings were practical people—best to hedge your bets.

+ JARL THE BAPTIST? +

Some Vikings had no problem getting baptized overseas, even if they never intended to give up the old gods. Baptism was often one of the conditions of making an alliance or signing a peace treaty in Christianized regions. Some Vikings even got baptized more than once. Why not, if it helped seal a deal? Bonus: the baptismal ceremony came with a feast and a brand-new white shirt—every time.

The Oseberg Grave Mound

The finest, richest ship burial in all of Scandinavia took place in Norway around 834. Two women were buried inside, one of whom had reached the unheard-of age of seventy or eighty years before dying of cancer, and the other just over fifty. Her cause of death is unknown, but Vikings were sometimes buried with a companion, presumably a slave who was killed for the burial. Clearly this was an important burial in their community;

this grave hoard is the largest ever found and contains the best examples we have of wood carving, furniture, sledges and wagons, clothing, and tapestries.

We can reconstruct the rituals thanks to careful archaeological work on the grave. The burial took at least four months. First, workers dug a trench up from the sea to drag the ship to the burial site—this happened in early spring, as plant-based evidence shows. Then a grave chamber was built behind the mast, and the stern of the ship was filled with food and cooking utensils, including a slaughtered ox. Then the back half of the ship was covered with a mound of dirt, giving the impression of a ship sailing down into the black earth.

Next the two women were laid in the grave chamber along with their fine possessions—and with a store of apples and bilberries, late-summer fruits in Norway. The final touch came with the sacrifice of ten horses and three dogs, whose heads were cut off on the foreship, drenched in a symbolic sea of blood. Then the front of the ship was covered in stones and earth to complete the mound, preserving it for more than a thousand years before it was excavated in 1904. The ship and grave goods are now on display at the Viking Ship Museum in Oslo, Norway.

+ AFTERLIVES +

Men who died in battle could hope to go to Odin's hall, Valhalla, but there's also talk of being welcomed by Freyja. Women also might go to Freyja after death, but unmarried women went to the minor goddess Gefion. If a Viking was particularly devoted to Thor or Frey, the god would protect his grave. Men who died at sea might go to the underwater hall of the obscure sea god and goddess Aegir and Ran. Those who died in bed would go to Hel's cold, misty realm of Niflheim.

Say what you will about Christianity, but the simplicity of heaven versus hell must have seemed refreshing.

RAGNARÖK: THE DOWNFALL OF THE GODS

All Hel Breaks Loose

In one of the most famous Old Norse poems ever written in the Viking Age, the *Völuspá* (The Seeress's Prophecy), a *völva*

or seeress born before the world began relates an epic vision of Ragnarök, the fate of the gods, telling of the destruction and rebirth of the world.

In the *Völuspá*, the seeress recounts the disasters as they begin to pile up. Baldur, second son of Odin and Frigg, was so wise, beautiful, and beloved that his mother forced everything on earth—animal, vegetable, and mineral—to take oaths not to kill him. With Baldur now seemingly invincible, the gods amuse themselves by shooting arrows and throwing rocks at him. But Loki finds a loophole: Frigg had overlooked the mistletoe plant, which seemed so harmless. Loki makes an arrow out of the soft stems and gets Baldur's blind brother, Hod, to shoot it at Baldur for fun. When the arrow hits, Baldur drops dead.

In revenge, the gods tie Loki to a stone with his own son's entrails and set a venomous snake to forever drip venom on his face. Loki's wife, Sigyn, stays by his side to catch the venom in a bowl, but every time she steps away to empty it, his agonies shake the roots of the world, causing earthquakes.

The death of Baldur is the first of many disasters that befall the gods and the world. "Hard it is in the world, there is much adultery, axe-age, sword-age, shields are cleft asunder, wind-age, wolf-age, before the world plunges headlong; no man will spare another." All the bound monsters break loose, and the sea rises over the land. A ship made from the finger-nails of dead men sets sail for Asgard, crewed by giants and steered by Loki. The fire giant Surt leads his kinsmen into the realm of the gods, shattering the rainbow bridge. Heimdall's horn calls the gods to meet the giants and monsters in this last great battle.

It's the End of the World as We Know It

Frey takes on the giant Surt, while Tyr faces the hound of the underworld, Garm. Odin battles the great wolf Fenrir, while Heimdall takes on Fenrir's father, Loki. Thor must face his old enemy, Jörmungand—he kills the serpent but then collapses and dies from its venomous bites. The wolf Fenrir devours Odin, and the god's son Vidar tears Fenrir apart to avenge his father. Heimdall and Loki kill each other; Tyr and Garm both die. Frey falls before Surt, and only the fire giant is left standing at the end to burn it all down. This is it: Ragnarök.

But at the very end of the poem, the seeress gives us a scene of hope: the earth rises from the waves again, and Baldur returns from the dead to rule with the surviving children of the gods. A man and a woman have survived among the roots of Yggdrasil to repopulate the world, and a new sun will outshine its mother in the heavens.

THE SUN BECOMES DARK.
EARTH SINKS IN THE SEA.
THE SHINING STARS SLIP
OUT OF THE SKY.
VAPOR AND FIRE RAGE
FIERCELY TOGETHER,
TILL THE LEAPING FLAME
LICKS HEAVEN ITSELF.

—*VÖLUSPÁ*

APPENDICES

LEARN MORE

APPENDIX I

TIMELINE

793   **ENGLAND:** Attack on the Lindisfarne monastery.

795   **SCOTLAND:** Vikings plunder the monastery on the island of Iona.

814   **FRANCE:** Emperor Charlemagne dies, succeeded by his son Louis the Pious.

833   **FRANCE:** Louis the Pious is deposed by his three sons, and the Frankish empire falls into disarray.

834   **NETHERLANDS:** Raid on the Frisian city of Dorestad on the Rhine River.

835   **FRANCE:** Attack on the monastery in Noirmoutier at the mouth of the Loire River.

841   **IRELAND:** Vikings build a fort at the Black Pool (*Dubh Linn*) to overwinter, which eventually becomes the trading center of Dublin.

844   **SPAIN:** Vikings attack Seville and hold the city for a week before the Moors drive them out.

844   **FRANCE:** Attack on Rouen on the Seine River.

845   **FRANCE:** Ragnar Hairy Breeches (Loðbrók) attacks Paris, farther up the Seine. Charles the

Bald pays the first of thirteen recorded Danegeld
payments in France, going up until 926.

845   GERMANY: Vikings plunder Hamburg.

859–862 MEDITERRANEAN: Bjørn and Hastein start
at the Loire River in France and raid Algeciras
in Spain, North Africa, southern Spain, up
the Rhone River to Arles, and on to Pisa in
Italy before returning home through the Strait
of Gibraltar.

860   ICELAND: Garðar the Swede explores Iceland, and
Vikings begin to settle there within a few years.

860   TURKEY: Swedish settlers in Eastern Europe,
known as the Rus, attack Constantinople for
the first time.

c. 862   RUSSIA: Riurik of the Rus founds a powerful
dynasty in Novgorod.

865   ENGLAND: First English payment of Danegeld, or
tribute, to the Vikings.

865   ENGLAND: Vikings make peace with East Anglia
in order to settle there and then expand their
holdings to York and onward to form the
Danelaw.

c. 880   NORWAY: Harald Finehair comes to power over a
unified Norway, and some disgruntled chieftains leave for Iceland.

902   **IRELAND:** The Irish expel the Vikings from Dublin.

911   **FRANCE:** Viking chieftain Rollo receives the territory of Normandy from Charles the Simple in exchange for defending the coast against other Vikings.

917   **IRELAND:** The Vikings retake Dublin.

930   **ICELAND:** The Icelandic Althing parliament first meets.

954   **ENGLAND:** The Danelaw kingdom comes to an end when King Eadred defeats the Viking king of York, Erik Bloodax.

c. 965 **DENMARK:** Harald Bluetooth converts Denmark to Christianity.

c. 980 **TURKEY:** The Varangian Guard forms in Constantinople, made up of Scandinavian mercenaries.

985   **GREENLAND:** Eirik the Red explores southern Greenland and starts a Viking settlement there.

983   **EASTERN EUROPE:** The Danes join forces with an alliance of Slavic peoples to push back the Germans.

991   **ENGLAND:** Olaf Tryggvason wins the Battle of Maldon.

1000   **ICELAND:** At the Althing, Iceland decides to convert to Christianity peacefully.

c. 1000   **NORTH AMERICA:** Leif Eirikson sails to Vinland.

1013   **ENGLAND:** Thorkell the Tall, a mercenary for King Aethelred, defends London from King Sweyn Forkbeard of Denmark.

1014   **IRELAND:** The Battle of Clontarf, where Brian Boru, high king of Ireland, defeated the Vikings and their Irish allies from Leinster.

1015   **NORWAY:** Olaf Haraldsson, later the patron saint of Norway, conquers Norway and declares it a Christian nation.

1016   **ENGLAND:** Sweyn Forkbeard's son Cnut is crowned king of England. He extends his power across Scandinavia, earning the title Cnut the Great.

1040   **MIDDLE EAST:** The Swedish chieftain Ingvar leads a failed expedition to the land of the Saracens.

1066   **ENGLAND:** William the Conqueror, a descendant of Rollo from Normandy, takes over England.

1085   **ENGLAND:** King Cnut of Denmark plans a mighty invasion of England that comes to nothing; it's the last Scandinavian effort against England.

1170   **IRELAND:** Anglo-Norman invaders take over Dublin, which had remained a Norse-speaking city until that point.

1171   **SCOTLAND:** Orkney Islands chieftain Sweyn Asleifarson, later called the last Viking, is killed in a raid on Dublin.

APPENDIX II

THE NEW VINLAND: VIKING ROAD TRIP

Where would a Viking feel most at home in the New World today? Here's a roundup of top destinations for a Viking-style getaway.

MOUNT HOREB, WISCONSIN

Welcome to the troll capital of the world, straight out of Norse mythology! Take the Trollway through the middle of town and try to count all the carved wood trolls in front of shops and cafés. If you visit in September, hit up the Thirsty Troll Brew Fest. Any other time of year, stop in to the Grumpy Troll Brew Pub and pick

up some "bean to bar" handcrafted chocolates at Sjölinds Chocolate House.

+ SIDE TRIP +

In summer, take the whole family to Troll Beach in Stoughton to splash around for the day and catch a performance by the famous high school group the Stoughton Norwegian Dancers. When the snow flies, bundle up for cross-country skiing in Lake Kegonsa State Park.

MINNEAPOLIS/SAINT PAUL, MINNESOTA

There's a lot to do in the Twin Cities besides going to a Minnesota Vikings game. Start at the American Swedish Institute, a museum and cultural center housed in a turreted mansion that offers language classes, craft and cooking workshops, and kids' activities. Or if you don't lean that way, get tickets to a talk, a concert, or an art show at Norway House.

When you're done studying, reward yourself with an Axe Man IPA at OG taproom Surly Brewing Company, or bring the kids and fur babies to HeadFlyer Brewing. More adventurous hop heads can sample the wild-yeast and farmhouse-style beers at Wild Mind Artisan Ales for a taste of how the Vikings

brewed. Swing by Ingebretsen's to stock up on Norwegian food specialties. Then cap off the evening with a gourmet dinner inspired by Scandinavian and Minnesotan food traditions at The Bachelor Farmer or Tullibee.

+ SIDE TRIP +

If you don't feel like deer hunting in the north woods, head south to Spring Grove, the first Scandinavian settlement in Minnesota. UffDa Fest happens every October, featuring a craft fair, beer garden, and live music at Viking Memorial Park and history and genealogy exhibits at Giants of the Earth Heritage Center.

MINOT, NORTH DAKOTA

If you're at least part Scandinavian, chances are you'll be invited to a family reunion in North Dakota at some point: the state has the highest percentage of people with Scandinavian ancestry in the United States, more than 36 percent. No visit to North Dakota would be complete without a trip to Scandinavian Heritage Park, an outdoor celebration of all five Nordic countries, featuring statues of Leif Eirikson and local heroes, a huge Swedish dala horse, and a full-size replica of a Norwegian stave church from the Middle Ages. Take it up a notch in September, when Dakotans flock to town for Norsk Høstfest, billed as "pure Scandimonium!" We hear  the cooks at the statewide Lefse Masters competition really go berserk.

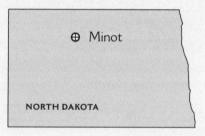

SEATTLE, WASHINGTON

Norwegian and Swedish immigrants felt right at home between the mountains and the sea in this Pacific Northwest town, many of them finding work in the fishing industry. Now it's home to the National Nordic Museum, a major destination for history

as well as modern Scandinavian art exhibits and music performances. In addition to downhill skiing, boating, and fishing, the city also boasts the largest *Syttende Mai* celebration in the world outside of Norway, honoring Norwegian Constitution Day with a parade and festival every May 17.

Let's not forget that Seattle is consistently one of the top cities in the United States for beer lovers, with more breweries than any other metropolitan area (174 and counting). And what pleases a Viking more than good ale?

+ SIDE TRIP +

Rent a sailboat or take a state ferry across Puget Sound for fjord-like views, and make your way to Poulsbo, known as Little Norway. Pick up some fresh *lefse* and *pepparkakor* at Sluys Poulsbo Bakery, or try the Valkyrie Red ale at Valhöll Brewing's kid- and dog-friendly tasting room.

PETERSBURG, ALASKA

Accessible only by sea and air, on a thickly forested island sur-rounded by mountains, Petersburg gives off a truly northern Norway vibe. Norwegians settled among the Tlingit tribe and established the fishing industry there in 1897, packing halibut and salmon in clear glacier ice. Today Petersburg is known for fishing, hunting, whale watching, and hiking in Tongass National Forest. Don't miss the Little Norway Festival celebrat-ing *Syttende Mai* each year, with Vikings and Valkyries roaming the streets, the Jormungandr Strongman contest, a parade, and much more. And it's only a ten-hour ferry ride from Juneau!

TOP VIKING MUSEUMS

SCANDINAVIA

THE VIKING SHIP MUSEUM
OSLO, NORWAY

View two of the world's most famous Viking ships, the Oseberg ship and the Gokstad ship, plus the remains of another long-ship and countless Viking treasures, housed in imposing white cathedral-like halls.

Website: https://www.khm.uio.no/english/visit-us/viking-ship -museum/

THE NATIONAL MUSEUM OF DENMARK
COPENHAGEN, DENMARK

Exhibits cover the Viking Age as well as the eras before and after, for a well-rounded view of Viking history. Browse online for an excellent, immersive look at many different aspects of life in the Viking Age. The National Museum also oversees historic

Viking sites, including the Trelleborg fortress and the monuments at Jelling.

Website: https://en.natmus.dk

THE VIKING SHIP MUSEUM
ROSKILDE, DENMARK

Sail on a re-created Viking ship and learn all about shipbuilding techniques at this beautiful waterfront museum.

Website: https://www.vikingeskibsmuseet.dk/en/

THE NATIONAL MUSEUM OF ICELAND
REYKJAVÍK, ICELAND

View the oldest known manuscripts of the Icelandic sagas at the Culture House, or Safnahús, and get a sense of how the original Viking colony evolved into a modern nation.

Website: https://www.thjodminjasafn.is/english

EUROPE

JORVIK VIKING CENTRE
YORK, UNITED KINGDOM

See re-creations of Viking buildings complete with animatronic Vikings and attend workshops in Viking crafts. Visit in February to experience the Jorvik Viking Festival.

Website: https://www.jorvikvikingcentre.co.uk

DUBLINIA
DUBLIN, IRELAND

Reenactors walk visitors through many different aspects of Viking and medieval life in Ireland. The National Museum of Ireland's archaeology exhibits are located just a few minutes' walk away.

Website: https://www.dublinia.ie

THE VIKING MUSEUM
HAITHABU, BUSDORF, GERMANY

Learn more about the Viking trading town of Hedeby, now part of modern Germany, at this UNESCO World Heritage site.

Website: https://haithabu.de/en/

NORTH AMERICA

L'ANSE AUX MEADOWS NATIONAL HISTORIC SITE
NEWFOUNDLAND, CANADA
Tour the archaeological remains of the only known Viking settlement in the New World, a UNESCO World Heritage site.

Website: https://www.pc.gc.ca/en/lhn-nhs/nl/meadows

NATIONAL NORDIC MUSEUM
SEATTLE, WASHINGTON, UNITED STATES
Formerly the Nordic Heritage Museum, the state-of-the-art building hosts historical exhibits as well as modern Scandinavian art and music events.

Website: https://www.nordicmuseum.org/

AMERICAN SWEDISH INSTITUTE
MINNEAPOLIS, MINNESOTA, UNITED STATES
The museum focuses on the Swedish immigrant experience in North America, with an extensive library for genealogical and cultural research.

Website: https://www.asimn.org

APPENDIX IV

FURTHER READING

Almgren, Bertil, et al. *The Viking*. Gothenburg: AB Nordbok, 1975. Published in the United States by Crown Publishers.

Crawford, Jackson, trans. and ed. *The Poetic Edda: Stories of the Norse Gods and Heroes*. Indianapolis: Hackett, 2015.

Davidson, H. R. Ellis. *Gods and Myths of Northern Europe*. London: Penguin, 1990.

Graham-Campbell, James. *The Viking World*. London: Frances Lincoln, 1980; New Haven: Ticknor and Fields, 1980.

Somerville, Angus A., and R. Andrew McDonald. *The Vikings and Their Age*. Toronto: University of Toronto, 2013.

Sturluson, Snorri. *The Prose Edda*. Translated by Jess Byock. London: Penguin, 2005.

Winroth, Anders. *The Age of the Vikings*. Princeton: Princeton University, 2014.

Zimmerman, Jereme. *Make Mead Like a Viking: Traditional Techniques for Brewing Natural, Wild-Fermented, Honey-Based Wines and Beers*. White River Junction, VT: Chelsea Green, 2015.